Magic As F*CK

By Jess at Those Phoenix Girls

Self-Written, Edited and Privately Distributed

Disclaimer

- "Those Phoenix Girls" is a trademarked brand and company as of 22nd February 2022. I do not give consent or rights for any individual or organisation to reprint, resell or use my work declared to be their own.

- All spells listed in the book have been practised by me personally. Spells can be very similar to the practises of other witches. Any similarities in spell methods or ingredients is simply coincidental. I do not claim to have owned or created all of the spells listed in this book. The spells listed are recommendations of my personal experience as a practising witch and can be altered to fit the individual person.

- Any actions taken by the reader is strictly on their own accord and within their own free will. I do not take responsibility for the actions of those who read this book. You are a free person to do as you wish, and all consequences of spell work are your own.

- This book is a guide of suggestions and personal experiences. It is not a factual manual of instruction. This is for entertainment purposes only and falls within the religious practise and spirituality category.

- While I am a qualified mental health professional, this book is not written as a mental health asset. The methods in this book should not replace your mental health treatment, although again you are a free person to do as you please.

- Any images used in this book were obtained free from Google stock images and WORD stock images. I do not claim to own them, and I believe to have full legal permission to use them to the best of my knowledge.

For the women that want more...

The women that have magic and fantasy in their veins...

The women who are tired of fighting for it...

The women that are ready for adventure...

For every warrior woman that is ready to experience ultimate abundance.

Thank you to the followers of **@ThosePhoenixGirls**.

You have carried and inspired me all the way.

A bit about me...

Hi, I'm Jess. I'm currently 27 years old. I have a seven-year-old son and a new baby daughter. I'm a qualified counsellor, mental health worker and women's rights activist. But the bit you're really interested in... I'm also a psychic. And a witch. I drive a Toyota though, found the brooms a bit sore on the cheeks. I suppose I could call myself a "witch" at this point, having managed to master spell work and manifestation. I certainly didn't get here without my fair share of fuck ups though. I won't bore you with my life story, but I will let you in on my gifts and how I've gotten to where I am now.

I knew I was different from a young age. I am a descendant of both Spanish and Irish witches who both practised witchcraft and mediumship. Probably from when I described my birth in perfect detail to my mum at just 2 years old. I could see and speak to people that weren't there. By the age of 7 I could see things before they happened, which was probably what scared me the most. For example, seeing my own swing snap while I was on it just seconds before it did. That was just one instance. I was always alone, I preferred to be. I seemed to attract people who were sick or vulnerable in my friendships, but I was also a dead set bulls eye target for bullies growing up. For some reason it felt like people just wanted to destroy me and I never understood why I kept to myself. It's still the same now at this age, I am constantly running into drama and hateful people. I knew that my life wasn't going to be an easy one when I started to accept my gift of seeing into the future. That unfortunately comes with its burdens. I am either loved or hated, I'm straight talking with an inability to lie or hide my true feelings and opinions. If you resonate with me, you're probably one of the gifted ones, too. I experience life in HD; I feel all, see all and "almost" know all. Not in a misogynistic way, it's just that I'm very rarely wrong when I see or feel something. Sometimes I wish I was.

Basically, I've managed to manifest pretty much everything I have ever wanted in life so far. It hasn't all been easy and its important you understand that. The spiritual path is a lonely one so be prepared to do a lot of things alone without the support or guidance of others. A lot of my clients have struggled going up against the judgement of others, so I always give them a little list of philosophy to follow:

- You only get one go at this life. You cannot rewind time or get these moments back. In the end, nobody's judgement will even matter. It's completely your decision on how you want to live this life as your physical being.

- Do no harm, take no shit. Be nice, be kind, be giving and be humble. But always stand your ground and never take shit from anybody.
- Choose your battles. Not everything requires a response or any energy from you. Keep the focus on you and your life from this moment moving forward; avoid the drama.
- You know what is best for you. Every single decision you make is meant to happen; you will never choose something that wasn't meant for you. Trust in your own direction.

Now be aware ladies. This book is not just a bunch of spells bundled together for you to try. This contains a lot of what I have learned about magic, manifesting and becoming the bionic woman. All scrunched and diluted to produce a small and easy read for you. You may even read this and think it's very limited, but in my experience, this is all you need to know as a beginner. People like to complicate things, there is money to be made in confusion and constantly dangling a carrot as if there is so much more to learn. Of course, you never stop learning in witchcraft. But these are the absolute basics you need to start on your journey, the rest is down to you to discover and work with. I have every faith that you can and will become the best version of yourself in this lifetime!

Do I know everything? Like fuck do I! Every day I am learning and testing our new ways to navigate this weird thing we call life. But I'm hopeful that this book can help you in some way. Enjoy!

Contents

Chapter 1 – Preparing for Magic!

Magic is everywhere. It's in all of us. As a woman, you are the definition of other-worldly magic. You can take a simple cell and create an entire human being in your body alone. You are the granddaughters of the witches they could not burn. You were born a magical being full of energy and power. As you grow older, society will start to drain your belief of magic and coerce you into a life that isn't meant for you. I'm going to show you how to unlock that inner goddess again, without all the bullshit in between. Just know this; you have had the power all along. You have it right now, just waiting to be awoken. So, let's do it!

Returning to Childhood

As a child, everything was magical. We literally believed we could fly using a few helium balloons, we wished on stars and swam like little mermaids. Nothing was impossible, imagination WAS reality. Do you remember how amazing life was? Wasn't it so much more colourful, exciting and liberating? Time passed slowly, love surrounded us, and the earth was ours to explore. As we age, the pressures of adult life begin to crush out the magic and replace it with stress, fatigue and routine. I used to get lost in books and films and they were my magical reality, nobody could tell me otherwise. Then I started to learn about death, evil and cruelty as I hit my teenage years. It was only when I had my son that I realised… I needed to get little Jess back. Your inner child is still very much alive within you, but she has been silenced. It's your job now to reach in and wake her up again. Without childlike belief in magic, there is no success in spell work. Your inner child is there every time you laugh, play, become amazed and dream. It is the part of you that experiences our physical existence to its absolute fullest… and it's still there.

Your understanding of what magic is, is very important. It's not like harry potter or Cinderella's fairy god mother. Magic is simply the manipulation of energy! All around you is magic. The birth of a baby, a life being saved, the moon and the stars. A spell is only a method of energetic manipulation, so it's important not to expect sparkles and fairies darting around the room when you start practising. In a nutshell, the key to manifestation and magic is *your belief and your intention.* So, let's have a look at how you can get back into your childlike energy and start making the magic happen.

- Dig out your old photo albums. Find a picture of yourself at an age when you felt the most carefree and happy. I would say this is anywhere between 7 and 11 years old. Sit with the pictures and reconnect with your younger self. Remember how it felt to be a child, what you might have been doing or thinking at the time and turn back the clocks. Take a good look at yourself and reconnect with the little lady within you, and she will say hello!

- Music! Old Disney songs and nostalgic movie theme tunes should spike the hairs on your arms and send you back to simpler days. Music has a frequency all of its own, and the power to heighten your vibrational energy. I have found that songs are the best method of restoring nostalgia. What were your childhood favourites? Get them playing and ignite those feelings again!

- Get lost in fantasy films and childhood movies. These films ignited imagination within us; do you remember desperately wanting to be the main character? Dressing up just like them, and damn well believing you WERE them? Do the same, try it out. Become a character for a day; that's why I go to Comicon's to become something much more magical. Be open to exploring life through a fantasy lense and nothing will be impossible!

- Create a Pinterest. This app has millions of amazing images that really highlight the beauty of fantasy and magic. Make a board for yourself including any pictures that bring you happiness, hope, nostalgia or a feeling of pure magic! Scroll through it once a day to keep the vibration moving.

- Play again. Go to the woods, go to the sea. Experience the life around you without stress or adult worries. Be present and take in all its wonders. Question everything, explore, create. Paint, draw, sing, dance. Become the authentic you again without worry of impressing anybody. And most importantly, detach from work and social media.

- Have a look at the messages we received as children. Disney for example, constantly told us about manifestation. "A dream is a wish your heart makes", "When you wish upon a star" and so much more. Fairies existed when we believed, in them and died when we did not. It's all a greater message; and as children we fully understood it. Go back and look and what they were trying to tell you!

- Idolise the right characters. Pocahontas and her strength and connection with the earth. Katniss Everdeen and her determination for truth, Mulan and her passion for unity.

Esmerelda and her quest for justice. Strong female roles were very present in our childhood; take another look at their stories.

Spend time around children too. Look at the wonder and innocence in their eyes. They are amazing at teaching us easy life can be if we just stop worrying all the time. Being a child ultimately is to be free from responsibility, having curiosity for the world, feeling no malice and enjoying life for the adventure that it is.

Ultimately what we are doing here is a factory reset. Removing the conditions of society, stress, boredom and being overworked. We are restoring your love for life and the earth around you. Once you can harness that inner child, you are capable of EVERYTHING. This is where the magic starts... when you believe again.

Removing Doubt!

What is doubt? A collection of fear, negativity and oppression. Doubt will be your downfall in both spell work and manifestation. If you hold onto pessimism, cancel the idea that magic will work in your favour. It works as a giant brick

wall against anything you may want to bring into your life. We only develop doubt as we get older and become disappointed with the world; it's not a natural emotion, its learned. 'I'll make this part short and sweet.

First, understand that magic and energy is constantly at work all around us. Coincidences aren't a thing, manifestation is. If you are new to this, we need to start opening your eyes to everything that's going on around you. At first it can be quite scary, to the point maybe it's easier to not have any belief in it. The biggest problem people have with believing in magic and manifestation is that you cannot physically see it. I suppose we as well have been conditioned as we have grown older that its nothing but a fairy tale. However, almost every single person who has practised magic or tried it out has seen its results! We can't see oxygen, but we know for sure it's there! Now you must apply the same understanding to magic and energy.

If you place an order on Amazon, you don't doubt that your order will arrive. You don't sit at your front door waiting for it either. You know it's on the way and you get on with your life. Sometimes we forget we have even ordered it until it turns up! Apply this energy to your spell work and watch how swiftly it is delivered.

It takes practise and persistence. But I assure you, as you start to watch your spells and manifestations come to fruition, your sense of doubt will fade away with your success. It's a life changing journey and nothing prepares you for the joy and excitement of realising how real magic is! As your confidence in magic grows, so will your power and your ability to manifest bigger and bigger each time. The key is, and always will be, complete trust in the universe and what it will deliver. Have faith, what have you got to lose?

Examples of manifestation you may not have noticed:

- Have you ever thought about somebody and then suddenly, they call, text or you bump into them? You manifested it!
- Have you ever started looking for a particular car and then suddenly the same car is showing up everywhere? Yes, you've manifested them!
- Have you ever accidently said "can you imagine if that item broke" and it did? Yep, you manifested it!
- Have you ever spoken about something totally random with somebody and then it starts showing up everywhere? You did it again!

Its been working constantly, except now you'll become more aware of it. And now, you can use it to your advantage. It IS real, trust that and work on removing your doubt!

Chapter 2 - Spiritual Development

A lot of people imagine a spiritual wakening to be an amazing and peaceful time in their lives. I can absolutely assure you that this will not be the case as you begin your spiritual journey to your higher self. It is absolutely worth it in the end; however, you are going to have to deal with your past traumas, painful memories and unlearn everything you think you know. Some of you may be wondering if you have begun your spiritual journey or how to start it at all. On the assumption that this is entirely new to you I will now be showing you ways to begin your journey and what to prepare for.

Ultimately this entire journey is a road to becoming your highest self. Your highest self is the version of you in the future that is completely designed and created by your human experience on this Earth. Your highest self is the version of you that you know you can and will become to the absolute best of your ability. She is strong, graceful and unaffected by the physical world around her. It's always helpful before beginning your spiritual journey to identify what it is you would like to become at the end of it all. Write out a list of qualities that you believe would be the best version of you to help you maintain a goal in this process. Always keep your eye on the prize and have full confidence in the guidance of the universe!

First and foremost you have to let both the universe and your spirit guides know that you are ready for your ascension to your highest self. You can do this by entering a meditative state and declaring that you are ready to begin your spiritual journey. Many people report feeling tingly and relieved after these words are spoken. It is best to do this at night before going to sleep as your spirit guides are likely to visit you in your dreams that same evening. Your guides may fully expose who they are, or they will drop subtle hints as to what is to come for you. If you are interested in meeting your spirit guides there are many amazing meditation tutorials on YouTube on how to do this. From this point onwards I advise that you do the following:

- Get a blank journal that you will now keep next to your bed. This will be used as your dream journal where you will document any vivid signs and scenarios that are shown to you within your dreams. This is because most of the time when you begin your spiritual journey you will start to be shown elements of your future that will soon become your reality. This is a very easy way of tracking your spiritual development and how often you are being shown parts of your future and others. Your subconscious is the window to another realm, pay attention to it!

- Begin to harness the power of manifestation using the law of attraction. I have explained this further in the next chapter. It is a simple way to start and begin this process by simply using your phone notes. Begin writing out small lists of things that you want to manifest into your day. This is an effective way of testing your energetic pull and your ability to manifest promptly and efficiently. Your phone is always on your person so that energy will be drawn to you naturally. Start small by manifesting random objects such as pink rabbits but you would not usually see in your daily life. This exercise will start to align you with the universe and open you up to the proof of manifestation working before your eyes.

- This is possibly one of the hardest parts of spiritual development, but it is absolutely necessary to guide you into becoming your highest self. You will need to keep another blank notebook that we are going to be calling your shadow work journal. Here you are going to be explore in the darkest elements of yourself and parts of you that you have been hiding from or avoiding. By exposing the parts of yourself that are hidden and traumatised you will then be able to heal them. This also includes any toxic traits that you yourself would like to clear and correct. This practice requires the ultimate sacrifice of your ego and nothing but pure honesty. It can be a challenging and emotional process but will indeed excel you into becoming the best possible version of yourself.

- Become consciously aware of your thoughts and feelings. This will help you to keep track of where you are at energetically. Start responding to people and situations rather than reacting. This will allow you to gain control over your own emotions and nobody around you will be able to influence that.

- Start spirit writing. Take some blank paper and a pen, close your eyes and ask your spirit guides to take control. Start allowing yourself to draw of write whatever you feel compelled to. This is your guides way of communicating with you. Always trust and believe what you have put on the paper, it is always a message.

- Be prepared to release all control and surrender your trust to the universe. There are going to be many scenarios that will be uncomfortable and possibly even painful. This is the universe's way of clearing out what is no longer serving you and you have to be able to trust that it's all for your highest good. Without trust in the universe and magic you will not be able to progress very far in your spiritual development. This can be difficult as you are relinquishing everything you have ever been taught but it is very much worth it.

Shadow Work

As I've just listed above, shadow work is an essential part of spiritual development. With everything in life, there is no light without darkness. You wouldn't be human if you did not possess a darker side; it's to embrace it rather than being ashamed of it. There is a lot of therapeutic detail to shadow work so I will do my best to keep this short and sweet. These are a few prompts that I have used to delve into my shadow self and assist me in reaching my highest self. You can find many more prompts and information on shadow work on Google and YouTube.

- What traits do you hate or strongly dislike about yourself? This is where you will need to be really honest with yourself in an effort to work on your most toxic traits. We all have them so it's important to work through the feelings of shame and guilt as you do so. For example, you might list that you tend to lie about things in your life. Hugh would then go back into your history and delve into the reasons for the lying. We have all had very different upbringings and some may include abuse and neglect. By being completely honest with yourself about your toxic traits you will be a step closer to reaching your full potential. Not only that, but you can also start to use your "flaws" as armour, rather than others being able to use them against you as a sword.

- What are your triggers? Think about any words phrases music or even places that trigger you. If you have been called names by people in the past what are they and why do they spur a reaction within you? For example, I was often called a drama Queen because my emotions were so intense. This word alone was a huge trigger for me and I managed to work through it by looking back at past events where it had shown up.

- What are your biggest regrets or parts of your life you would love to go back and change? Ask yourself what you would have done differently with the knowledge you have now. This practice allows you to deal with regrets of the past and identify how much you have grown since that time. Being honest about your mistakes is a fantastic way of owning your past and moving forward into your prosperous future.

- What are you worried about that people may think of you? Explore what parts of yourself you worry that people may notice and discuss amongst themselves. Find out why it is that you care what others think. What would you think of yourself from an outsider's perspective?

- At what points in your life did you suffer abuse or injustice? Look at how those scenarios may have affected you to this day. When we carry post-traumatic stress, it can impact our entire personalities and the way we view ourselves and our lives. Use this time to look at what you endured and how much you may still be carrying with you. Work on releasing those memories and dealing with what you endured.

These are just a few pointers for shadow work and as I have mentioned there are many more resources you can find online. In doing shadow work which I recommend doing once a week you will start to build a barrier of pure bionic energy. Once you are able to identify the parts of yourself you dislike, not a human being on this planet can then use it against you to hurt you. Embrace your shadow self as part of your armour against the world as you move forward.

Harsh truths you need to face...

- Not everybody is going to like you. In becoming your highest self, you will indefinitely make some enemies along the way. People will indeed try to diminish your light and prevent you from progressing. Get comfortable with being disliked and embrace confrontation when necessary.

You are going to 'lose' friends, family members and partners. Anybody that your spirit guides deem a threat to your spiritual progression will be removed from your life immediately. To many this comes as quite a shock and can put them into dark Places. Understand that these removals are for your highest good and will protect you in the long run. Before spiritual awakening we are unaware of toxic individuals around us. On this journey you will become crystal clear about who has good intentions and who does not.

- You will have to bury the past version of yourself. In spiritual ascension there is no room for weakness. Your spirit guides will actively be working to toughen you up to the world around you. This means that you must trust in what they are showing you and embrace the growing version of you. Everything you once thought you knew about yourself, let it go. You are about to be shown what you really are underneath years of social conditioning.

- You have "toxic traits". You aren't perfect and you never will be. At this point you need to own them, and I'll be showing you how. Acceptance of your entire self will create the bionic woman within you.

How to handle the Bullshit!

So, it's all hit you pretty hard. Your boyfriend of five years just left people you classed as your best friends have shown some true colours... you're feeling lonely. You're feeling as though you might be the problem. Yep, it can get rough. But let me assure you that you are exactly where you are meant to be right now.

"Out with the old, in with the new". It's true to its phrase. If something in your house is too old, breaks or it's just not your style anymore, you throw it out. It's a bit harder with the people in your life, I get that. Most of us stay stuck in toxic relationships and friendships because we build genuine connections, create memories and nostalgia and of course, create a future with these people in our minds. There are huge chords attached and it can hurt like hell when they are suddenly severed. There is no denying that loss of any kind is tough, but in becoming your highest self, detachment from certain people is simply unavoidable. It's like removing an apple from a bowl of rotten ones to protect its health. And that's exactly what will happen to you, ultimate and divine spiritual protection! Trust that your spirit guides have got your back. Trust that better friends are just around the corner. Trust that your ex was not the one for you and the universe will soon guide you to meet your soul mate. TRUST, TRUST AND MORE TRUST. Use this experience of purification to be specific about the kind of people you now want in your life.

Confrontation will absolutely arise. Everywhere, at any time, with anyone. Now that you are on a path of enlightenment, you will certainly find yourself under attack from darker and lower energies. You will now be a threat to those who are jealous of your light, unable to understand it or just plainly want to destroy it. Be sure of yourself in every sense. Who you are, what you believe, what your reality is and what you stand for. At this stage in your journey, you need to be fully aware of manipulation and gaslighting from narcissistic individuals around you. And trust me, it will show up everywhere.

DON'T TAKE THINGS PERSONALLY. How a person behaves and treats you says everything about them, and nothing about you. Nobody really cares that much about you to judge you; they are all too busy judging themselves and trying to turn their negativity on others.

Understand that it really isn't about you. Most of the time if someone hates you, it's out of jealousy or you trigger something within them. Sometimes if somebody doesn't love you, it doesn't mean you aren't loveable, it means they aren't capable of love. Even if your parents weren't great to you, it's absolutely nothing to do with you, it was their \own internal issues that were reflected in their parenting. This can be hard to come to terms with, but once you release the burden of believing you are the problem, you get rid of most of your insecurities.

Beware the radicals!

As a witch, you will become a target of radical religious groups. People in general may call you crazy or weird but don't worry, they're just scared of you. Christians (radical ones) will indefinitely attack you. You will be called the spawn of Satan and told you will burn in hell for your evil acts. Understand one thing; these people are severely mentally ill and are not to be taken seriously. You will come up against all kinds of criticism, people fear what they cannot understand. Also, they know full well how powerful witches are, otherwise they wouldn't waste time trying to destroy you. My best advice is do not engage. They will goad you and question you, but no matter how well you express your argument, it is literally talking to a brick wall. Reacting will only give them the negative energy they desire to thrive on. Leave them to it and get on with your shit. Besides, in my opinion its all the same thing. Some call it god, we call it the universe. Some call it prayer, we call it manifesting. Either way, we are all accessing the source of power and energy! Respect all faiths, but also expect it in return.

Dealing with Break ups...

Now, I know this isn't a book on love and relationships. BUT, by now I'm pretty sure 90% of the problem for women is recovering from break ups with men that couldn't see how lucky they were. This issue seems to be the main barrier for women becoming their highest selves. Especially when dealing with narcissistic individuals who quite literally fuck up our entire sense of being. Obviously, there is so much attached to a relationship and all of this is easier said than done, but here's a few things I want you to know:

- They always come back. Really, they do, Whether its tomorrow or next year. They always come back. Most of the time its curiosity or testing whether they can get you back. It will very rarely be the last time you ever see or hear from them. You had a connection and connections don't just disappear.

- Relax, don't panic. Having a break can actually be an amazing part of any relationship. It reignites passion and appreciation for each other. Space is important for reflection and growth so leave them be to get into their feelings. In the meantime, work on building yourself and become comfortable alone.

- Have faith in the universe. What is meant for you will never pass you. If he is the one, he will be back. If he isn't, then you'll meet the one soon enough. No amount of stress will change anything, trust the process!

Always remember that some people come into our life for a season, for a lesson or by total accident. Not everyone we meet is meant to stay on our path. Understand that YOU are a huge loss to your ex-partner. Focus on you and then they show up! As a spiritually awoken woman, you will attract lovers that need healing, and this can be draining. Remember not to take on the problems of others as your own.

**I have written this from my own perception as a straight female. Please adjust the pronouns and genders to suit your orientation"*

Spirit of the Wolf

The wolf is notoriously known for its strength in both its packs and in its solidarity. When you get into the world of witchcraft, you have to be ready to embrace the spirit of the wolf. In a nutshell, you need to be prepared to stand tall and walk your own path. People will start to show a lot of true colours when you evolve spiritually, and you must be prepared for it. This is all part of the bigger plan; low vibrational people will immediately start to be removed from your life at an alarming rate. Becoming a witch, goddess, or simply your highest self requires an incredibly thick skin. I wish I had known this years ago and how liberating it is to simply tell people to fuck off. As women, we have a tendency to mother and see the best in people. This can leave us stranded with individuals that use and abuse us. Often, there's a lot of fear connected to letting people go. Being comfortable, or the worry of the unknown. And of course, the panic of being lonely.

As you begin your spiritual journey, you will indeed learn that you are never alone. Your spirit guides, ancestors and supporting goddesses will be with you every step of the way.

Your power comes from within. As generic as it sounds, it's true.

While this journey is not an easy one, you will live a more

fulfilled life and experience much more than many ever will. Once you understand your abilities, your powers will only multiply.

Now is the time to become best friends with yourself. It sounds strange, and maybe a bit pathetic, but trust me it will change your entire life. Have you ever found yourself literally talking to… yourself? Do you always feel that you're never truly alone? That's because you aren't. The voice in your head is you, just later on down the line. The voice that tells you not to do something is your highest self-intervening. It's the voice that comforts you when things get tough, and the voice that motivates and pushes you to achieve something. Your biggest fan, your best friend and the one person who will never let you down, is yourself. And its time you start to realise that, rather than putting yourself down the way society wants you to.

Have you ever noticed how EVERYTHING is about changing ourselves? Whether its weight loss, make up, hair extensions, lip fillers… it's all about becoming what we ARENT. Isn't it funny that if you hear "voices" you are diagnosed insane? The voices, however, are just your highest self and your team of spirit guides! But they don't WANT you to know this! Having low self esteem makes money, oppresses your vibration and keeps you reliant on societies standards. Break out of the matrix and become unapologetically, yourself.

Tips to keeping your energy vibration high!

- Understand that you only get one shot at this life. You will look back on the days you spent doing nothing or miserable and wish that you had them back. Look back at the days you were upset over an ex; don't you wish you could change them now?

- Worrying changes nothing. Read that again. Stressing over anything doesn't change the outcome, in fact if anything it could just make things worse. Consciously remind yourself that stress and worry will have no positive impact on your life.

- Dance! Sing! Shake off negative energy and create new heightened vibrations with your voice and your body! Music can change your feelings in a split second. Choose happiness!

- Deliberately spend time with people who you feel are on your level and make you feel good. People that can hold a conversation, care for your feelings and validate you should you need it. You are who you surround yourself with, so keep your standards high.

- LAUGH. Yes, laugh your fucking head off. Belly laughing is without a doubt the easiest way to manifest something quickly because the vibrations around you are so high! I usually watch fails on YouTube or indulge in comedy. It will indefinitely shift the energy around you.

Understand that it is perfectly normal to have down days and negative emotions, that's just part of being a human being. Those days won't affect your long-term goals and manifestations as long as you don't fester into darkness. Embrace those days and release them. Emotions do not control you, simply observe them and send them on their way! The practises you have just read will take time to master, but repetition breeds routine. Actively remain focused on improving yourself and elevating your spiritual spirits and I promise, you will never look back. If you're going to need a therapist, find someone spiritual who you feel you can trust (and of course won't rob you blind with extortionate prices). Look after your body with good foods and engage in exercise every now and then. Its all about YOU from this point on.

Chapter 3 – Universal Laws

I probably don't need to lecture you on the fact that there are universal laws. While there are actually 12 universal laws, there are seven that I focus on and apply to my spell work. You can have a little google of universal laws in more detail if you're interested in learning more about them! Here is a very general run down as follows:

1 – **The Great Law.** Also known as the law of cause and effect, what goes around will surely come back around. The most basic understanding of Karma.

2 – **The Law of Growth.** This law focuses on expansion within the universe. Growth will never and can never be stopped. Growth of energy, growth within ourselves, and of course of nature.

3 – **The Law of Force.** This energetic law can prevent you from investing into too many things at once. It literally forces you to put your energies into where they are needed. It will also force the division of yourself and something that is not meant for you.

4 – **The Law of Creation.** As the name suggests, this law is all about our energetic creation! It encourages us to go out and get what we want, make our dreams a reality rather than sitting around and waiting for it.

5 – **The Law of Responsibility.** This law urges us to be aware of the consequences of our own actions. We must always take responsibility for ourselves and our decisions. We must also not take on the responsibility of others that does not belong to us.

6 – **The Law of Giving.** We must never act in greed. What you receive from the universe, you must also give back. Giving to others boosts and aligns your own karma. Taking too much from the world around you will result in loss.

7 – **The Law of Vibration** – The notion that literally everything on this earth has its own vibration. This can be high or low functioning and you attract whatever energies you are vibrating out into the universe. This is a scientifically proven fact of nature.

The Three Laws I Practise: Karmic Law (The Great Law)

So, karma is actually a big thing. It may not hit straight away or in the most obvious of ways, but it is constantly at work. One of the most important things you need to ensure as a new witch, is that your karmic energy is balanced. We can't have all good karma, that's impossible. Sometimes we do shitty things and that's cool! But you have to be aware of the fact that without good karma to balance it, bad things may come to you. So, first and foremost, let's get your good karma up to scratch.

- Do something nice for somebody once a day. It doesn't have to be huge. Make it a mission to give a compliment or do a favour for someone every day and watch your vibration rise.

- Choose how you respond to difficult situations and people. I am guilty of road rage and flying off the handle but try to approach everything and everyone with love and patience. This is fantastic karma, every nasty word that isn't spoken is a gold star on your chart.

- Do things for free, pay for something for somebody or just do a kind deed for someone less fortunate than yourself.

- Be kind to animals and children… big one. We have to protect the vulnerable and those that rely on us. Abusing anything or anyone that is defenceless is seriously frowned upon.

Donate to charities or help the homeless. The universe is constantly presenting us with opportunities to help the less fortunate. Next time you see a homeless person or a chance to donate to a charity, take it. The universe will reward you thoroughly.

Remember this: What I give out comes back to me times three.

This will take you time to grasp, but soon enough you'll start to understand how your karmic scales are weighing up. Signs of bad karmic energy include arguments, accidents, money losses, breakages, injuries, low mood and general bad luck. Signs of good karmic energy include money increases, affection from others, peaceful moods, lucky occurrences and good health. Have a little look at your daily life and measure up before doing any spell work. We can ALWAYS improve and make up for any bad decisions!

Karma in Spell Work

Don't ever do a spell on somebody without their permission. The only times you can do this is when somebody has fallen ill and needs healing or if it is a child in need of good health. Otherwise, stay clear of it. Even if you think you are doing the right thing, karma will disagree with you. There are ways around this of course, but you have to be clever about it. I've included some examples of bad karma in spell work that could lead to a nasty backlash:

- Doing curses or hexes on somebody that is weaker than you, pregnant or sick. Absolutely NO GO. Also, do not curse or hex anyone without justified cause to do so. Only return the same level of pain or disrespect to them that they gave to you.

- Putting love spells on people that are already in a relationship. Trust me, don't even try it. I can assure you it will backfire, and you will never have what you want from the situation.

- Doing money spells out of greed. Only use spell work when you are in need, not for greed. Keep that information with you and you will always be abundant.

- Using money spells in gambling, for example to win the lottery, roulette or bets. This is never a good idea and can be seen as manipulating energy in a negative way for personal gain.

- Doing a spell to get someone out of an abusive relationship or workplace. While this seems like a good idea, it goes against free will and will have some consequences on your part.

Ultimately, it's your call when doing karmic spells. You have to be sure that your target deserves what is coming to them and it isn't done out of hurt or spite.

You can build amazing karma by practising health spells, especially on children. As long as you know what you are doing and your intentions are pure, you will continue to raise your vibration and activate your heart chakra.

Law of Attraction

This is one of the most magical and important universal laws in spell work. Manifestation means to create your own reality simply from a thought or an idea. The law of attraction explains how you have an energy field of your own and the ability to draw in what you are focusing on. Absolutely everything that comes into our lives is a direct consequence of what we think and feel. It is happening constantly to all of us. What we put out into the universe is what we receive back! I will explain in the best way I can how to use this law to get exactly what you want and need from life.

The Power of Gratitude

Now you may have read in books such as "The Secret" that gratitude plays a powerful part in manifestation. I can confirm, it does. Sometimes we focus so much on the negatives in our lives and what we don't have, rather than valuing everything we do. There are a few energetic reasons why having gratitude is so important:

- It gets you into a happier and more positive mindset. Focusing on problems and what you lack in life will propel you into low vibrations. Reminding yourself of how lucky you are and what you already do possess will change your outlook on your present and elevate your vibrational energy.

- The universe loves to keep giving when it knows its work its appreciated. For example, if you bought someone a gift and they showed no appreciation for it, you'd be unlikely to buy them anything again.

However, if that person showed complete gratitude and happiness with your gift, you would want to give more! The law of attraction works in the same way.

You attract what you are. If you are miserable, pessimistic and negative, you'll inevitably attract more of that. If you are positive, upbeat and happy, you'll attract more of it. Become what you want to attract. I understand that this is easier said than done, but once you understand that moping around really gains and changes nothing, you'll automatically start being more positive.

Many of you will have watched my lives and by now, should know the type of person I am. I do not believe in toxic positivity. It is physically impossible to be positive and happy all of the time. Dedicate an hour of your day to feeling your sadness, anger and negativity before releasing it into the universe. As long as you understand that those feelings are totally normal and they don't control you, you will soon be able to put positive thoughts at the fore front of your subconscious. Allow yourself to be imperfect, to have down days and bad moments and then your body and soul will be able to release it and allow in light energy!

Placing an order with the universe...

Now that we have removed your doubts, it's time to put your full trust into the universe. The first step to doing this is by placing your order! Yes, literally. When you make an order on amazon, you don't doubt that it will turn up, do you? You make your order and then get on with your life. Sometimes you even forget you've ordered something until it turns up at your door. THIS IS THE KEY! Releasing your order into the trusting hands of the universe speeds up your manifestation massively. Obsessing over it or dwelling on doubts and negative thoughts will just postpone its arrival or destroy it all together.

There are a few ways to place your orders and ensure that the universe is fully aware of what you want. First of all, be careful what you wish for. Not everything you think you want is a blessing and may bring with it a lot of negative energy. For example, manifesting your ex back. It's totally possible to do this, however it does not mean that they will have changed in any way. Think about why your relationship ended in the first place and never manifest an abusive person back into your life. It will only get worse, and I'm speaking from experience. We all have free will even when our paths are destined.

Then, you need to give the universe a leg up. If you're looking to manifest money windfalls, you need to put yourself in a position to obtain it. Start applying for new jobs, buy scratch cards etc. If you're looking for love, get back out there. Go on dating sites. Unless your soulmate works for Amazon or Hermes, prince charming isn't going to rock up at your door. With every action you take, the universe will respond with a reaction. Start actively turning the wheels so that the universe can work alongside you.

So, place your order. Be certain on what it is you want and send it off to the universe to accept. Let go of the need to control how your manifestation will arrive and just trust. Do little steps every day to work towards your goal and always throw positive energy towards it. Have patience, don't lose faith and watch for the signs around you. I use a manifestation book to do this, I call it my magic pages where everything I write inside it comes true! I also use dragons blood ink to speed up the process. Above all, have fun with the process and become excited about what your life can and will become!

TIP – Always attract with need, never with greed. You will read this a few times in this book, but its absolutely true. Greed is a no go, and you could end up losing more. Start small and work your way up.

Law of Connection

This is a commonly overlooked and disregarding law of universal energies, but without a doubt one of the most powerful and important to consider in magic and manifestation.

We are one. All of us, everything. Every plant, animal, insect, human being, energetic force is all connected. Every move that is made affects each and every one of us. This energy is constantly moving throughout the universe and can be manipulated to suit any individual.

Looking at all of these laws can be confusing, but once you get a basic understanding, your knowledge of it will only continue to grow. Look at the way the world works for example. The water evaporates and becomes rain clouds, only to start the cycle all over again. Every action has a reaction, every movement has a consequence. The man having a bad day who can't get his car into gear at the traffic lights, then delays everybody else's day. Those individual people then impact others, and so it continues. Everything is connected.

When you are using magic and manifestation, you have to be aware of the energy surrounding of everything and everyone involved in your manifestation. Always state at the end of any spell, "may it harm none". This ensures that if for example you are asking for a money windfall, that it doesn't take the money away from somebody else. Always consider the impact your spells will have on others to avoid karmic backlash and respect the universal laws. It's also important to understand that the actions of others could be impacting your spells or manifestation. For example, somebody may be manifesting the exact same job position you applied for! It happens, but the universe will always deliver what belongs to you. Someone could also be manifesting YOU. This becomes clear when you start to randomly think about someone a lot, they show up in your dreams and you have a strong urge to contact them!

I recommend studying all of the universal laws to get a bit of an idea how our universe works. The three laws listed above are the laws I practise heavily in spell work, but you may find that you work more closely with any of the others. Always do your own research and practises!

You are never alone. You are the entire universe.

Chapter 4 – Lets Make Some Magic!

So now that you've mastered your mindset, we can start having some fun with spell work. I have selected the easiest, quickest and most effective spells I have ever used for you all. Let's face it, were busy. We don't have time to be searching for crazy ingredients or waiting for the moons phases to change. You can do these spells anytime, anywhere. You may even think "really, that's it?" Yep. Magic really isn't complicated, and you will soon learn this. All that matters in spell work is the power of your intention; everything else involved is just a bonus! Have confidence, enjoy experimenting with magic and remember to follow the steps I have listed previously in the book. You'll do great!

The spells I will be listing here are some of the easiest and most efficient spells I have ever used. If you follow my spell page on Instagram **(@PhoenixSpellWork)** you would have seen hundreds of results from these exact spells. However, there are some personal spells of mine that I use that I won't be listing. This is because it has taken me over 10 years to perfect these spells and any newbies attempting them has the potential to go horribly wrong! So, I will still be available to do personal spells for you all with my own rituals if you need it.

As you start trying out some spells of your own, remember the three keys:

1 – **Trust.** Be fully invested in your intention and trust that the universe WILL deliver. Have patience and remain positive.

2 – **Release.** Let go of your spell or manifestation and get on with your life. Obsession is a block so do your thing and then let it go.

3 – **Record & Receive.** Make a note of the signs the universe gives you that your wish is on the way. Note down how long each spell took to show results. And of course, record the actual result of your spell!

Welcome to the world of witching, ladies. Once you begin, you never really go back. So, get ready for a whole new world to open up before your very eyes!

Calling in Goddesses

As you probably know, goddesses have existed throughout history across all cultures and religions. There are Greek, roman, Egyptian, Celtic, Hindu, elemental and many more goddesses. It would probably take me months to sit here and list them all so I'm going to make it simple for you guys. To call upon goddesses, simply light a candle and set up the offerings required. Then ask them to assist you in your spell work. Your candle will usually flicker if they accept your offer.

These are the goddesses I call upon in my spell work and what they are best to assist with:

Venus - goddess of femininity, love, sex and passion. Venus is best called upon for self-love, physical beauty, abundance and romantic attention. She accepts offerings of gold, milk or honey.

Aphrodite - Goddess of fertility and child protection. She is best used in fertility spells, pregnancy protection and protecting children from abuse or bullying. Offerings of chocolate, candles and roses.

Hecate - Goddess of Witchcraft and manifesting. She will enhance your spell work. Offerings of earth, pomegranate and dried herbs.

Lakshmi- Hindu goddess of money and fortune. She is best used for money spells that involve large amounts of lucky windfalls. She accepts offering of yellow flowers and coins.

Athena - Goddess of War, Strength and protection. Offering of wine bread or olives. She is best used for emotional healing, determination and willpower.

Justitia - Goddess of justice and law. She is best used to assist you in legal battles and up against official scenarios. She accepts offerings of old jewellery and citrus.

Khali (many spellings) – Hindu Goddess of karma and male punishment. She is best used in karmic spells, particularly against males. Offerings of gold coins, red flowers or red wine.

Hygeia- Goddess of Health and Medicine. She is fantastic for any health spells. Offerings of fresh fruit and green vegetables.

Yemaya – Goddess of the ocean and fertility. She will assist with any conception spells. Offerings of semen (yuck I know), seashells and plums.

Clementia – Goddess of reconciliation and forgiveness. Offerings of white flowers and honey.

Medusa – Goddess of Sexual Protection. She is best used in healing sexual or vaginal infections, protecting your feminine energy and gaining sexual power over men. She accepts offerings of cranberry, silver and grey stones.

The amazing thing about working with goddesses is that they welcome all, regardless of your status. They are non-judgemental and exist to serve women throughout the generations. Each goddess carries with her the stories of thousands of young women, the energy created, and it is a continuous loop of magic. The only times a goddess will not work with a woman is if she is cruel at heart and lives to harm or destroy others. If you were that type of woman, you wouldn't be reading this so don't worry yourself. Learn about them, embrace them and inhabit their powers as they work alongside you! Above all, always give offerings and gratitude to our goddesses as they carry us through our spiritual journeys. They are our ancestors, our teachers and our protectors. Trust in them and they will always deliver.

Zodiac & Elements

The stars and the planets have huge effects on us! I am not an astrology witch, but I know for a fact that fucking mercury retrograde does us all in. Do a bit of studying on the planetary impacts on earth and it may help you with your own work. Your zodiac sign says more about you than you may think. No doubt all of you have done some digging into your star signs, especially if you've been watching my weekly horoscope readings! But aside from the personality traits, each of you have a soul that belongs to one of the four elements of the earth. Those are Water, Fire, Earth and Air. You can apply your elemental connection to your magical practices, and it will enhance your powers and your results!

WATER: Scorpio, Pisces & Cancer

Using water in spells is very simple and effective. Water signs can use jar spells, bath rituals, lake and sea water. Use blue crystals to support your element and water spirits will assist you if you chose to manifest by water in nature. Your element is free flowing so your magic naturally will be gentle, going with the flow of the universe. Water signs are naturally adaptive to change and this gives spell work the ability to go where it needs to.

Other relations: *Neptune, The Ocean, Change, Protection, Song, Mental Health, Fertility.*

FIRE: Aries, Sagittarius & Leo

As a fire sign, you are guided by passion and the fuel of your heart. Logic isn't something fire signs tend to use often! Using fire in spells is extremely effective and speeds up the energy surrounding your intention. Bonfires are absolutely incredible for manifesting and rituals; the energy is just paramount! Candle work is incredibly powerful when conducted by fire signs as it engages and harnesses your energy from something as small, yet destructive, as a simple flame. As a fire sign, you are most powerful during phases of anger and orgasm (yes, you read that right). Apply it!

Other relations: *Mars, Venus, Love, Passion, War, Strength, Lust, Persistence.*

EARTH: Taurus, Virgo & Capricorn

Earth signs tend to be very grounded and logical. Naturally you will think deeply about what you want to achieve without acting on impulse. This is a fantastic trait to have as a witch as we must always be careful what we wish for, so use it! You will work well in the woods, with plants, herbs and all things natural. I also recommend Earth signs work with water as it aids their element in growth and adaptation.

Other relations: *Saturn, Jupiter, Mother Earth, Health, Money, Stability, Growth, Recovery.*

AIR: Gemini, Libra & Aquarius

Air signs are very skilled at adjusting to changes in life. Air is a fuel element, and your energy is used to enhance spell work and manifestation. The best days for you to do spell work is during a storm or an extremely windy one; your vibrations will be sky high! Always get outside and somewhere open such as a field or the beach to access air in its most powerful form. You will work well with all of the above elements in an outdoor environment.

Other relations: *Adapting, Truth, Conflict, Mercury, Moving on, Destruction, Messages, Karma.*

You can incorporate any of the elements into your spells and after some practise, you will know exactly which element to use and when. Trust your own judgement and above all, have fun with the earth's powers!

Crystals & Magical Items

You all probably know enough about crystals at this point and of course, can access so much more information about them on the internet. I'm just going to quickly give you a rundown of types of crystals and items I use and what they attract:

Attracting Love – Rose Quartz, Clear Quartz, Red Jasper.

Attracting Money – Citrine, Amethyst, Clear Quartz, Pyrite.

Attracting Health – Amber, Aquamarine, Jade, Malachite.

Protection – Black tourmaline, Obsidian, Evil Eye.

Pregnancy – Coral, Rose Quartz, Seashells.

Healing – Moonstone, Sea Glass, Rose Quartz.

Clarity and Motivation – Tigers Eye, Clear Quartz.

Psychic ability – Amethyst Point!

With crystals and magical items, you can use them however they work best for you. Although they all have their own properties and powers, crystals are adaptive to their owners and the intentions set upon them. It's the same with herbs. Rosemary is fantastic for love spells but many of my witchy friends prefer to use it in health spells! It all depends on what feels right and what calls to you. This is why I'm not doing too much coverage on magical items because every witch has her own way! There are many fantastic books on crystals and their uses, and of course, Google and YouTube. Crystals tend to choose their owners so when buying them, always go where you are drawn, and you will find a magical assistant.

WARNING!

You may have seen a lot about moldavite "magically" changing people's lives and becoming hyped up on social media. Moldavite is a very powerful space rock that has the ability to shift out energies completely. Yes, this will change your life but if you aren't ready for these changes it was cause absolute havoc and destruction within your life. It has also been known to cause psychotic episodes and hallucinations. I personally would avoid this stone at all costs. Even as an experienced witch, I refuse to bring something into my life that will scramble everything, and I will lose control completely!

Moon Phases

The moon is incredibly powerful. She governs our feminine energy and even controls our menstrual cycles. While the sun is masculine energy, the Moon is entirely representative of Women! We are made up mostly of water and that is what the moon impacts on earth! Human beings of all cultures have worshipped the moon since the beginning of time. She is a force to be reckoned with and will most definitely support you as a growing witch! I will very briefly give you an idea on the phases of the moon and the energy it will contribute to spells and manifesting:

Full Moon – This phase is fantastic for manifesting and enhancing any spell work. Fertility spells are always best done on a full moon as it represents new beginnings, creation and cycle completion. This moon is also known to cause chaotic energies, mostly in women! Personally, I avoid doing any long drives or big days out on a full moon as the roads are usually hectic and people behave out of character. There is a reason people say the crazies are out on a full moon!

New Moon – This phase carries with it a bundle of emotional phases of its own. Many people describe feeling more tearful, angry and reflective on a new moon. However, this moon helps to release the stresses of the previous month and restart you in facing the next. Karmic and Love spells are best done on a new moon as people are more open and receptive to energies.

Waxing Gibbous – This phase is all about productivity, money and luck. The energy is stable, settled and full of motivation. Any spell work done on a waxing gibbous moon will be slow but progressive. This is the ideal phase for money and luck spells, including taking any tests or doing interviews.

Waning Gibbous – This phase is best used for decision making, enjoying life and spontaneity. I often use this moon phase to create new opportunities, find new friends and draw in excitement. Abundance and motivated spells are best done during this phase.

Remember that you are your own witch and never to follow spell books as a bible, more as a guide. You will soon develop your own relationship with the cycles of the moon. You may find that the full moon is best for releasing rather than creating. It is different for us all! If you are a total beginner, start using the phases as I have explained above. Then, as you progress, harness the phases of the moon in your own way and what works best for you!

Cleansing and Protection

Many witches prefer to cleanse and protect their energy before doing any spell work. You can also use the following tools to cleanse your home. If this is something you would like to do, I recommend using the following:

- Palo Santo sticks (burn and smudge)
- White Sage (burn and smudge)
- Incense (burn, smudge and cleanse)
- Himalayan Salt (add to diffuser or bath)
- Black Obsidian (keep on person)

You can research the protective properties of these items further if you wish. There is a lot to it, but just know they are all fantastic for cleansing, clearing and protection. I strongly recommend burning bay leaves in spell work. Not only do they make *everything* happen, but they release protective energy as they do so!

Right, I think that's it. Are we ready to practise some spells?

Let's go!

Love Spells

I mean... we all want to love and be loved, right? But sometimes, negative energy and factors can get in the way of things. And sometimes, people need a push into clearer thinking when it comes to love.
I use these spells to attract love, heal wounds in my relationships and return an ex to me if I feel we have unfinished business. These spells do not mess with free will. If the person in question has genuine love and care for you, these spells WILL work! Love is a powerful emotion and I truly believe it never really goes away. You can use these spells as you wish but try to focus on drawing in what is best for you and everyone involved.

WARNING! Karmically, doing spells on a person that is in a relationship will have dire consequences. Avoid this at all costs. Especially if their partner is pregnant as interfering with the beginning of a new life is very much frowned upon by universal energies. It is also my personal advice to never do love spells on an abusive ex-partner, as when they return, so will the abuse. Nothing will change.

Honey Jars

This is one of the simpler spell techniques to sweeten things up with you and your loved one. This also works with friends and family members. It is one of my favourite and most effective spells to sweeten up relationships and relax conflict.

You will need:

An empty jar with no labels

Pure bees honey

Sugar

Chocolate powder

Rose petals

Rose oil

Cinnamon

Pink candle

Rose quartz

All things sweet!

Write both of your names on a piece of paper and circle the names clockwise. As you fold the paper towards you three times, speak out clearly your intentions for this spell. For example: "John will contact me within 3 days and resolve this argument"

Place the folded paper at the bottom of the jar. Now start to add the honey, make it a layer thick enough to cover the paper. Then begin to add the sugar, oils, petals and sweet stuff. I usually play some Disney or love songs in the background as I go! I visualise them getting into contact with me and what I want them to say. Once everything is added, seal the jar lid with the wax of a pink candle. Place a Rose quartz on top of the jar and leave by your front door to welcome them back in.

Job done!

"Picture Perfect" spell

This is a very simple but effective spell to get somebody to contact you. You will need a picture of your person looking directly at the camera, as if you are holding eye contact. Pictures in happy places or in a happy memory are much better to use. I always say the more recent the photo the better, and even more powerful if you took it yourself!

Sit for a few minutes and connect with the picture as if you are in front of them. Ask them to come home, to call you or message you. Declare that all obstacles between you be removed. Printed photos work better but just using your phone is fine!

Then let it go. It's that simple. By speaking to your person, you are forming a cosmic connection and they will soon receive your message telepathically. You can light a candle if you wish, but I've had huge results just from this practise alone.

"Growing Love"

This is a spell that I created by myself one day in October 2021. A friend of mine had recently separated from her husband of five years and desperately wanted to fix it. That night I had a dream distinctively showing a rose bud growing at a fast pace from a plant pot. I took it as a sign to begin producing a new love spell! I concocted this design combining a few factors from my other spells, but something about this one felt raw and powerful to use. I realised; their love hadn't died at all. It just needed a boost, and indeed, to grow again. So that's exactly what we are about to do! You can use this spell if you are single and looking for love, need a romantic boost in your relationship or if you are trying to reignite an old spark.

You will need:

- A plant pot or jar
- Soil
- Paper and pen
- Seeds of any kind
- Water
- Red wine (optional)

This is best done mid-afternoon on a sunny day, but any weather is fine. First, take your plant pot or jar and fill it halfway with soil. You can use soil from your garden if need be. Then write down the name of the person on the paper. Cross your name on top of their name three times. Fold the paper three times towards you saying "come to me" as you do. Then put the paper into the jar and cover it with the rest of the soil. Red wine is amazing for love spells so if you have some lying around, pour some on top of the soil in a clockwise motion. If it's a jar, seal it with a lid but pierce some holes. Take your jar or plant pot outside near your home and bury it. If you can't dig a hole, set it down somewhere in the woods and keep it hidden. As you leave it, ask the universe to grow the love between you and your person. And you're all done! You can choose to revisit and keep watering it, but it isn't absolutely necessary.

"Close to my heart"

Very simple but very effective mini spell. Simply write the person's name you want to hear from on a small piece of paper. Circle the name three times clockwise and as you do, speak the following words:

"I bind you to my heart, expose your true self to me. By the power of three, so mote it be, and may it harm none". You can also directly ask them to contact you and speak to them as if they were in front of you.

Then fold the paper towards you three times and place it in your bra on your left side close to your heart. You should get communication from this person within seven days. If no communication comes in, burn the paper and release it to the universe. Your person will either show up or you can let it go completely.

Forever Together

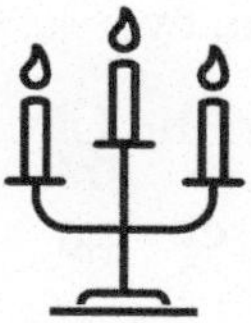

This spell requires the consent of both parties before it is carried out. DON'T attempt to do this without their knowledge as it will backfire karmically and end in disaster. Be certain of your decision to dedicate your love to this person as these spells are tricky to undo!

You will need:

- An empty jar
- A Candle wick or String
- Candle Wax
- Hair strands (yours and theirs)
- Nail clippings
- Pink Himalayan Salt
- Sugar
- Honey

Take your empty jar and place the candle wick into it. Start heating up your candle wax and add the above ingredients. It doesn't matter what order you do this, just do it with the intention of combining your spirits with love and protection. The hair strands can be tied together or left loose, as long as you have both of yours in there. Mix it all up together. Both of you pour the wax into the candle and say, "Ever thine, ever mine, ever ours". Its one of my favourite quotes from Sex and the City and I soon realised how powerful it was! Allow the candle to set. Any time your relationship goes through hardship, light the candle and the sweetness and love will soon be reignited between you.

TIP!

When doing love spells, always remember that free will is at play. So don't expect everyone to fall at your feet when doing these spells. However, if there is serious potential there and that person has feelings for you, these spells will work every time! Play some love songs whenever you are manifesting love as its about the feeling that comes with it that brings it to reality!

The Famous Venus Spell

The Venus spell is my most successful and requested spell from clients. This spell is a combination of many things, but the main effect is the goddess energy that empowers femininity. It is activated using a phrase and the energy can last for up to 14 days. Some clients of mine have also reported this spell lasting for over a month. Although there are many variations of goddess spells, I've customised this spell to attract love, money and success all at once! I recommend doing this spell once a month to continue attracting your desires. It's also a perfect pick me up when things seem glum or hopeless.

Venus is the roman goddess of love, feminine power and abundance. She is the epitome of beauty and attracts everyone around her, particularly men. There are plenty of goddess' that represent similar attributes, but Venus is one that always delivers when I call on her. When making offerings to Venus, there are a few things you should know. She is incredibly generous and playful; her favourite colours are pink and red to represent love and lust. She favours the harp and loves pomegranate. In the past I have left pomegranate seeds out as an offering to Venus and within hours they all began to disappear! Ask and you shall receive, literally. This spell is best done on a Wednesday, regardless of the time or moon phase.

You will need:

- A clean bowl
- Paper and pink/red pen
- Dried rose petals or fresh flowers
- Fresh fruit (pomegranate, orange, peaches, strawberries)
- Virgin olive oil
- Perfume or scent representing love
- Gold coin (pound coin, cents etc)
- Dried herb (coriander, oregano, rosemary)

First, set up your spell mixing bowl. It doesn't matter what you use here as long as it's clean and large enough for the ingredients. I always recommend putting on some high energy music that focuses on female empowerment as you do this spell. Wear an item of pink or red to draw in femininity and offer Venus some fruit by your bowl. Add all of the above ingredients together, leaving the gold coin and perfume to the side. As you mix it, call upon Venus to fill your life with abundance, love and health. You should start to feel light and tingly as she accepts your offering. Place the bowl of ingredients in your garden or somewhere in nature. Take the gold coin and kiss it, thanking Venus for her help before you throw it into the bowl. Then spray your chosen perfume three times over the bowl and three times on your neck. Take a deep breath, close your eyes and vocally announce "VENUS AWAKEN". You're all set! Leave it there for 14 days for the spell to brew and watch the magic come swiftly into your life!

I have hundreds of reviews for the Venus spell on Instagram that have brought so many miracles into people's lives. Try it for yourself and remember to record your results!

Making Love & Lust Oil

This oil is very simple to make but it has powerful properties. I recommend using it on your pulse points and only applying it within 7 days of making it. Use this oil on first dates, around somebody you are interested in or on a night out to become irresistible to a man's senses!

You will need:

- Rose Hip Oil
- Dried Rose Buds
- Cinnamon
- The juice of any red berry

- Sprig of rosemary
- Olive Oil

Mix all of these ingredients together while listening to your favourite love songs. Get the romantic or sexual energy going as you create it. It doesn't matter how much of the ingredients you use; this is your personal oil so it's totally your combination choice. Bottle it, store in a cupboard and apply when needed! (Lust oil goes on the neck and inner thighs but you probably already guessed that!)

Fertility Magic

One thing that saddens me to my core is a woman struggling to conceive, grow or raise a child of her own. I see this level of pain, I have felt it also, and I know just how much fertility issues can destroy the soul of a person. I am passionate about a woman's right to motherhood and I believe those struggling should have access to help without it costing thousands in time, money and energy. I personally struggled with fertility for five years and have lost two babies in the womb without explanation. Having a daughter was my dream, so I devised a magical "plan" to get what I want and deserve. As I write this, my daughter is currently smiling away at 4 months old. It is entirely possible to conceive using magic and I currently have had 117 successful pregnancies from my spells. Below I will list the most powerful fertility spells and tools I have used to conceive and have shared with others who have had the same results! Please be aware that there are some circumstances in which even spell work will not be successful, and they are: sterilisation, transgender females, two ovaries that do not produce eggs and polycystic ovaries can be a struggle. Biology is unfortunately also an important part of fertility spell work that we cannot always change. Taking all of this into consideration, we can start manifesting a baby!

Full Moon Ritual

The moon is a symbol of femininity and fertility; a woman's cycles follows that of the moon! Many women have learned to actually sync their menstrual cycles with the moon to enhance fertility and maintain control of their hormones. Doing fertility spells on a full moon is a winner; I have had an 82% success rate with my clients for all full moon rituals. This particular ritual helped me to conceive not once, but TWICE! I now swear by it to all who are trying to conceive.

You will need:

3 Candles (Pink or Red)

Lighter or Matches

Paper and pens

Transport

On a full moon, take a drive with your partner. Take with you 3 candles, pen and paper. First, drive to the mothers chosen place that reminds her of happy times as a child. Light the first candle and ask the universe to grant you the opportunity to be a mother. Leave it to burn somewhere protected from wind. Then drive to the place where your partner spent his childhood. Get him to light the second candle and ask for the opportunity to become a father. Again, leave the candle somewhere safe to burn. Finally, drive to a location that you feel represents your relationship (where you first met for example). Both of you light the last candle and thank the universe for allowing you to come together and create another life. Leave it in a safe place to burn and off you go!

Fake it till you make it!

Manifesting is all part of the process. The best way to create something into your own reality is to put it there! Fake it till you make it... literally.

Get a pregnancy test and pee on it, as you do. If it's positive, congratulations! But you won't be needing to do this. Get a red pen and draw another line onto the negative test making it appear positive. Feel the feelings of getting a REAL positive test. Then, leave the test somewhere you will see it every day. Eventually, the positive test will manifest itself into your reality while you train your body into pregnancy.

Start taking pregnancy vitamins. It will do absolutely no harm to your body and will in fact help prepare your womb for your little one. By taking these vitamins, you are physically and mentally training your body into preparing for pregnancy.

Remove any negative emotions associated with pregnancy. Stress is a massive block to conception, and this is where most people fuck up. Relax and trust that your baby is coming. I advise not to do any tracking, thousands of tests before your period or any actions that harness negative energy on pregnancy. Forget all about it and get on with your life. Then, your baby will show up. Easier said than done I know, but just trust me! If you look at the tribes of the Earth, their population rate is so huge. I believe most of this is because the women do not stress themselves about getting pregnant and they just do! Your body was made to do this so trust it.

Making Fertility Oil

Best made three nights before the full moon, this oil has helped so many of my followers to conceive. I used this oil twice before getting pregnant with my daughter.

You will need:

- Olive Oil
- Pine needles
- Dried rose buds
- Cinnamon
- Rose hip Oil
- Crushed folic acid

Take a clean bowl and fill it with pure virgin olive oil. Add a few stems of pine needles, the fresher the better. You can also place pine needles under your mattress for fertility magic. Add the petals of the dried rose buds one by one, keeping the image of pregnancy within your mind. Cinnamon adds passion which aids the conception process so tip in a bit of that! Rose hip oil is about love and connection so add a few drops. And of course, folic acid is the main vitamin needed to maintain a healthy pregnancy. Once you've stirred up your oil, rub your hands together and hold them open over your oil. Say the following out loud:

"Goddess of the moon, sun, earth and stars... bless me with a healthy child within three cycles. I am fertile, my womb is ready to house this baby"

Then let it sit for 24 hours and rub it on your abdomen before having sex. I recommend only using this once a week and be sure you aren't allergic to the ingredients. So, as well as physically aiding your body in fertility, its full of magic and intention! Trust, believe, and your baby will soon be with you. You can always make more and remember that your baby will show up at the exact divine timing. Try not to put a time scale on things and focus positive healing energy into your womb.

The Mermaid Jar

This spell is fantastic! Not only are the results incredible but it really is one of the most magical spells a woman can experience. Although all of the fertility spells I use are effective, I found this spell to be the winner in conceiving my daughter. Only 18 days after I created the mermaid jar, I got my positive test! It's also an incredible experience to work with mermaids and will indeed fill you with hope and magic.

You will need:

An empty glass Jar

Sea water

Shells

Paper and Pen

Tea light candle

Take an empty glass jar down to the sea. You can do this during the day, but I prefer going at night as I can actually hear siren song when its quiet! Sit peacefully and imagine your womb filling up with golden light. Write out a letter to your future baby; explain why you deserve them and the kind of life you will give them. Keep the images in your mind of having a baby and everything you want to happen. Then take your jar and fill it with sea water. Collect some shells from the shore that you are drawn too and add them into the jar. Ask the mermaids to bless you with a healthy pregnancy by the next full moon (the universe loves specifics!). Sit back down and light your candle, writing out a letter to your future baby asking them to join you in this life. Thank the mermaids for their assistance before rolling up the paper and placing it into the jar. Seal the jar tight and then drip the candle wax clockwise over the lid of the jar. Then bury your jar deep into the sand, the further into the seashore line the better. Take a few minutes to ground yourself and feel the excitement of you baby that will soon be coming to you. Wave goodbye to the mermaids, thank them and off you go!

Testimony

Just wanted to say thank you so much to Jess. She knew my struggles and I said to her "why not?" When she asked me if I wanted to try it? I had nothing to lose. I lost my first baby back in October last year and I was so close to giving up. It broke me!! Jess did the fertility spell on me, and I found out in my next cycle that I was pregnant. I remember sitting on the toilet for about half hour not believing what I could see on the pregnancy test.

I found out I was 3 weeks, and I was so excited, but so nervous. Fast forward to now, we found out we are having a baby girl in December and we are over halfway. What makes it crazier is that me and Jess are having our babies a few days apart! Absolutely mind blown.

Thank you so much again Jess!

Charlotte C, London

Amazingly, Charlotte and I ended up giving birth on the exact same day, 12 days early in the same hospital! Both of our babies were included in the same fertility spell.

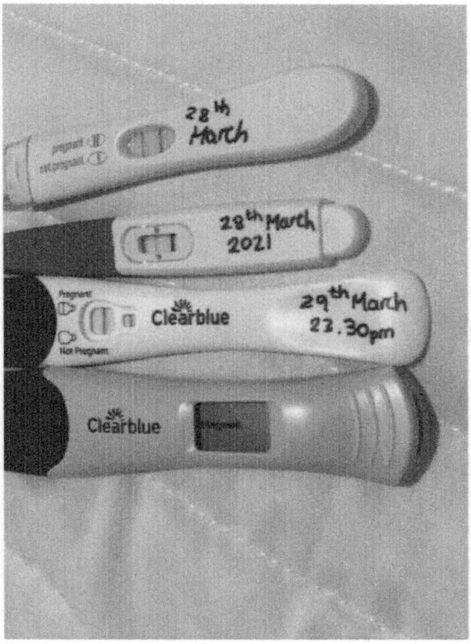

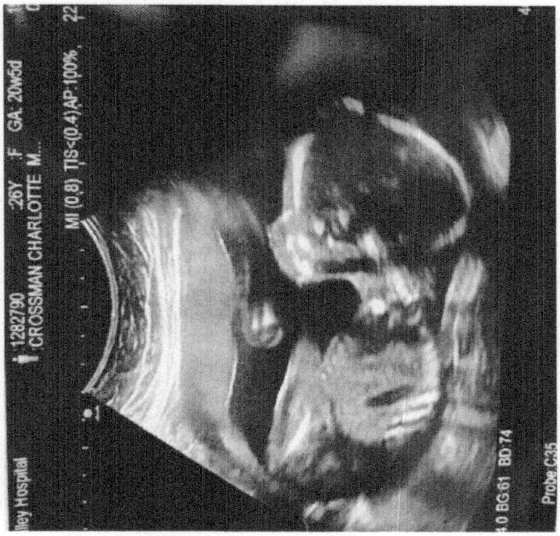

This is just one of 117 results. You can find the other pregnancy spell reviews on my Instagram!

Health Spells

Your health is primary. If you aren't healthy, everything around you will fall apart. It's important to be in the best condition you possibly can, so I've put together a few spells to help you maintain your human form.

Use your hands!

Yes, we can heal with our hands. This is best done on somebody else. Slowly move your open hands over the affected area. Imagine you are bundling up black smoke from underneath them. Drag the black smoke from out of their body and will it to leave them. Then wash your hands. Go back and imagine gold light flowing from your hands replacing where the black smoke once was. Keep telling their body to heal over and over and it shall!

The other way of doing it is very aggressively telling the illness to fuck off and demand that is leaves immediately. Worked for me and many others I have done this for!

Weight Loss

This spell is very efficient but does require some work and patience. You don't need to take out a gym membership or change your diet, which is a perk. You do however need to be dedicated to this spell to get the best results.

Lemon has been used in weight management for centuries. The citric acid targets and burns excess fat in the body in a natural way. I don't recommend eating lemons excessively as it can cause reflux and tooth erosion, but it is necessary for this spell.

You will need:

- Lemons!
- Pen and paper
- Citrus essential oil (lemon/lime/orange)
- White or green candle
- Ribbon of any colour

Eat one lemon every one to two days. I recommend cutting it into pieces and eating the juicy bits with the skin. Don't eat the exterior skin, this makes no difference and doesn't taste great! This is part of the spell but also a great physical method to shed the pounds in a short amount of time.

Write down your desired weight and stick it on your scales. If you don't have scales, put it on your fridge or somewhere you can see it. This will manifest it into your reality.

These spells work best on Sunday evenings. Fill your kitchen or bathroom sink with water, make sure the plug is in. Add your citrus essential oils and swirl the water clockwise. Light your candle and put it next to you in the bathroom or on the windowsill. Anoint the candle with the same essential oil and leave to burn. Place both of your hands in the sink, close your eyes and take a deep breath. Recite the following:

"My body is under my control. As this water drains, remove the toxins and tone my body. My will be done, so mote it be"

Pull the plug from the drain and hold your hands in the water. Allow the water to flow away and imagine it is dragging out black fluid from your body. The weight is literally draining away...
Wave out your candle, thank the universe and your spell is done! Be aware this spell requires patience as results can take time to notice.

And yes, EAT THE DAMN LEMONS. Spoon it out, do not mix with water as it won't work!

AVOID this spell if you have citrus allergies, eating disorders or are currently pregnant.

Athena Align!

This spell is a recent ritual I have been practising that relieves anxiety, depression and heartache. It also supplies its target with emotional strength and bursts of motivation. I have had fantastic results from this spell and could not wait to share it with you all!

You will need:

- A Mirror
- An Incense stick
- Pure Sea salt
- Water
- An offering for Athena (see goddesses' chapter)

First, light the incense of your choice and stand in front of the mirror. Raise your shoulders and tense all of your muscles for 10 seconds. Release and take a deep breath. Call upon Athena to deliver you her strength and stability. Now, look deep into your own eyes until you enter a trance state. You should start to zone out and your mind will go blank. As you do, start to chant the following:

"Power within me, power surround me!"

Once you feel it's time to break connection with your soul, step back from the mirror and smear water across it. This is an act of cleansing yourself while projecting your emotions onto the mirror. Then, take the salt and sprinkle it once around your head clockwise. Thank Athena for her assistance, shake your body and then go and rest. You should feel completely at ease for the next week at the very least.

General Health Spell

This is more of a ritual than a spell but has always worked for me when I need a health boost. For this you will only need one potato! It will sound crazy but carry your chosen potato around with you for 24 hours. This potato will act as a sponge for illness and draw it out of your system. As you go on through the day, start cutting off pieces. Discard them and say, "thank you for providing me with health". When you finally get to sleep, cut the potato into two slices and place them in your socks. When you wake, discard them and have a bath in just warm water (no soaps). You should feel much better!

Money Spells and Manifestation

Before we start, I first want you to understand what money is. Copper, silver and a bit of paper. Don't put too much energy into obsessing over money or you will continue to block its arrival. It is nothing more than a physical item and it doesn't deserve the amount of power it holds over you that it has. That being said, we all need it to survive. So, I'm going to show you how to effortlessly attract money into your life.

Mindset is key. "Money does not control me, I control money". Never give anything the ability to control you or it will indeed spiral out of your control. Take ownership. Believing that you are broke or in debt will only attract more of that. From this moment onwards, money is nothing more than object that you can easily obtain. You DESERVE money. You deserve financial stability and comfort. Money comes in weird and wonderful ways when using spells to attract it. You may be given lots of free stuff, discounts, gifts from others at the very least. On the bigger scale, clients of mine have had big lottery wins, been given new jobs and even received large pay outs and inheritance. It really depends on what the universe has planned, but you can always attract money no matter what your fate holds.

Flip a coin!

Let's start off nice and simple. All you need for this is a coin, doesn't matter whether its silver, copper or gold in colour. Face it heads up on your thumb and flick it into the air. As you do, say "my luck shall turn, money flows to me now". Do this three times and keep the coin on your person, in your bag or in your car. This is also the most powerful luck spell there is, and it will turn the tables. Very easy and very effective!

Welcome, Welcome!

Very easy spell this one! Many cultures use this practise as a way to welcome good fortune and financial stability into their lives. The frog is a symbol in my cultures of abundance and financial success. You may recall seeing metal frogs in the corners of people's homes once or twice in your lifetime. This method is similar. Draw a frog or obtain a statue of a frog and place it by your front door. Surround the frog with copper coins in a circle and leave it for as long as possible!

Cheque In!

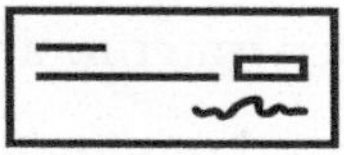

You may have heard of this manifestation technique in the book "The Secret". While it's not exactly the same, it is similar. All you need to do is get a blank cheque or piece of paper. Write down the exact figure you want to attract and put it somewhere you can see it. I always put them on the fridge as I visit it a lot! You can also keep it on your person until it arrives. This number then becomes engrained in your subconscious and you will naturally attract it!

Money Simmer Pot

This is a method I have used for many years and keeps your finances stable with gradual increases over time. It comes from a Spanish and Mexican background but can be used by anybody!

You will need:

- Citrus (Orange, Lemon or Lime)
- Fresh Mint

- Coriander
- Yellow Flower petals (optional)
- Copper Coins
- Ylang Ylang Oil
- Cooking Pot

Get your clean cooking pot and add a good amount of boiled water to it. Set the intention that this ritual will create financial stability and money influx over the next 30 days. Cut up two citrus fruits into sliced and add them into the pot. Dash some fresh mint, coriander yellow flower petals into the mix. If you have ylang ylang oil, add a few drops as this oil is fantastic for money attraction and speeding up spell work. Stir clockwise and repeat the following as you add 5 copper coins:

"Money arrives, it remains and grows. Abundant in money as this energy flows. Thank you for the money I receive and the money I am yet to receive".

Then leave it to simmer on your stove for one hour. Once finished, you can bottle it or pour it outside the front of your house to welcome money into your life. Results will be slow and steady, but I have seen some cases of this spell bringing in large sums of money very quickly. It all depends on what you need and how you manifest it!

Buried Treasure

Anyone for a pirate adventure? Take a gold coin and plant it outside or in a pot. Water it once a day and urge your finances to grow! Simple, yet incredibly effective. Intention is everything!

When doing money spells, it's important to remove negative attachments to it. Don't speak out words such as "broke" or "debt". Do not consume your thoughts with money and it will arrive. As always, have full trust that the universe will deliver what you need!

Interviews & New Jobs

First of all, get a very clear idea of the type of job you want. Where is it? What is the pay rate? How many hours? The more specific you are, the quicker you will manifest it into your life. Write all of this down, fold the paper towards you three times and keep it under your pillow. I always put a penny in the envelope as a money magnet too. If you already have the interview. Write out an email or letter to yourself from the company in question stating that you got the job! Keep it on your fridge or somewhere in sight and you will manifest that exact email into your reality! Taking pyrite to an interview ensures confidence and success so I would recommend this. Affirmations for this would be as follows:

- I am the best possible person for this job, and they know it.
- This interview is already going in my favour.
- I already have won the job position.
- Thank you for handing me this job, universe!
- This job was made just for me and I'm here to claim it.
- Financial security is falling into my hands as we speak!

Confidence in key in all walks of life, especially when you feel the need to prove yourself somehow. Always trust in the universe and your spirit guides will carry you through it effortlessly.

Again, you can find all of my money spell reviews on Instagram. I've actually lost count of how many successes I've had at this point, but I know I've now got three files full of them! These spells are powerful, but your mindset towards money will be the key to the outcome. Remember the tips I have provided and enjoy seeing what your magic can do!

Protection, Releasing & Karma Spells

As a spiritual being, you will encounter many foul people on your journey. This ranges from narcissists, psychopaths and deranged individuals, right through to jealous and generally annoying people. I certainly have made a few enemies along the way, and I'm glad I did. It means I stood up for something. If you don't have enemies, you aren't being true to yourself. That's what I believe anyway! So, obviously I've had to come up with ways to get rid of these people and keep them away. The world is crawling with them, so knowing these techniques will keep your circle safe and protected from their bullshit energy.

Freeze that bitch.

Got a bad neighbour? A spiteful old friend? A crazy ex that just won't leave you be? Time to freeze these bitches. And its dead easy! It stops contact and harassment almost instantly.

You will need:

- A Jar (preferably plastic as glass can smash when frozen)
- Water
- Paper

- Pen
- Picture of them (optional)
- Pepper corns
- Salt

First, clean your jar out properly. You don't really want any leftover dolmio going on with this spell. Could accidently spice things up a bit! You can also cleanse it using incense or sage but that's not really necessary. Once your jar is clean, put it to one side. Take your paper and pen and write the name or names of the people you want to block out of your life. Write on top of their names the word "BLOCKED" three times. Fold the paper three times away from you and place it at the bottom of the jar. Circle some salt three times anti clockwise on top of the paper to keep you protected from them. Then, if they've been really nasty, add a few pepper corns to send their negativity back to them.

Fill the jar with water and seal it shut. I usually seal all jars with candle wax but that isn't a necessity with this spell. Put it in the bottom or back of your freezer. Shut the door and say, "you are now blocked from my life, good riddance and good will". That way, karma is on your side as you are wishing them no harm but removing them from your life is absolutely your right. Leave the jar in there until they have been gone for a significant amount of time and showing no signs of returning.

Reverse that shit.

Are you suddenly having strings of bad luck? Overwhelming negative thoughts that you know are not yours? Everything seems to be falling apart? It's likely that someone is sending you negative energy or even trying to hex you. Fear not, we can send that shit back and times it by ten. They'll regret trying to mess with you once they get a taste of their own medicine!

You will need:

- A handheld mirror (one sided)
- A white or black candle.
- Incense or sage.
- Table/Sea salt.

Many people like to sage or light incense before doing this ritual. Take your candle and light it. Sprinkle the flame with sea salt and ask that you are protected and purified during this ritual. Take your handheld mirror and position is against your chest facing outwards. Simply say "Whatever negative energy has been sent to me, I send it back by the power of three". Then turn three times in a circle anticlockwise to undo the hex or evil eye. Sprinkle some salt onto the mirror and then wipe clean to cleanse it before using it again. This will work within hours and your life will return to normal!

Purification Bath

Water is of course fantastic for cleansing. It is the elemental used in all cultures to purify people, items and places. Baths are so sacred they are even used for baptism! The best way to get rid of unwanted energy is to simply wash it off!

Run a bath as hot as you can stand it (without causing burns or discomfort) and close all windows and doors to allow the room to steam. Add pure sea salt or Himalayan salt to the bath. You can also use something called "blue" which is a protection tool. Get in and scrub your skin as if you are scrubbing off black filth. Literally imagine you are cleaning yourself of the shit that has happened recently. Lay there for a few minutes and then pull the plug. Remain in the bath as the water drains around you and imagine all of that black fluid is draining away. Once it's all gone, take your shower and run it over yourself quickly. Imagine gold light restoring your energy and luck! And you're done!

Bitch, Bye!

This is such a simple but effective ritual to remove somebody from your life, even your thoughts. Write the name on a piece of tissue paper and flush it down the toilet after finishing your business! You are literally flushing that person from your life. Easy, job done.

Protecting Children

Sadly, we live in a world where other children aren't always so nice. Bullies exist at school and on social media. To protect your little ones, when they are asleep go to them in their beds and do the following:

Hover both of your hands over your child. One over the head and the other over their heart. Close your eyes and take a deep breath. Imagine gold light flowing out of your hands and creating a shield around your child. Chant the following:

"Any who try to harm you shall be turned from you. Their words stolen from their mouths and their targets placed elsewhere. You are shielded from all harm, sadness and panic. Gods and Goddesses surround this child with your armour and hold them in your divine energy. Thank you, thank you, Thank you".

Then rub your hands together and go to wash them as if you are removing any negativity energy that was within them or surrounding them. You can also use dreamcatchers to remove negative thoughts (they do actually work!). I have put a black obsidian crystal in my son's school bag or coat pocket and he never had any trouble after that.

Children are naturally protected as they are innocent, but sometimes they will require some help. Understand that in most cases your spells will work without any karmic backlash and 99% of the time, they are perfectly fine to do. I would advise asking permission from them if they are old enough, just to be clear/

Karmic Spells

We have all been screwed over one way or another in our lifetimes. After a lot of practise and research, I have come to understand that we can take karma into our own hands. Refer back to the law of karma when practising these spells and rituals.

In simple terms, you can only practise these methods if you have been deeply violated. Only ever ask for an equal dose of karma unto the person who has wronged you. For example, if somebody stole £5000 from you, ask that the individual suffers a loss of this exact amount, no more and no less. Its very likely that they will be hit harder, but don't ask for it and the universe will deliver. Many witches avoid hexing, but in 2022, we are surrounded by some seriously evil bastards. And in my opinion, why should they get away with it? Being the bigger person was never really my style, so here are a collection of my most efficient karma spells! Use with caution please ladies and always for justice, never out of spite!

Sour Jar

Yep, clue is in the name. We're going to make a jar full of disgusting shit. Now this spell is only for the worst of the worst, it's not too short of a curse. It's up to you to decide if its karmically justified, but I would personally only use this spell on abusers, r*pists and p*dophiles. It can however be used for thieves who steal huge amounts of money from you or seriously damage your property (like burning your house down).

You will need:

- An empty jar (glass only)
- Pen and Paper
- Pepper corns
- Chili (fresh or powder)
- Mustard or Spices
- Lemon or Lime
- Fish that has gone off!
- Anything disgusting you can find!

Yeah, when I said sour jar, I meant absolutely vile jar. Slugs, snails and puppy dogs' tails... we all remember that one. So first get your jar. Clear your space, its best to do this outside to avoid dragging negative energy into your home. Write their name and push it the bottom of the jar. Then fill it with all of the disgusting things you can find while remaining in your state of anger. Crush it all up together and then take the jar from your home to be buried. I usually spit on it once I've buried it but I'm petty, It's an option though! And that's it all these is to it. This is probably the spell with the quickest results and is my go-to method.

Salty Sender

This spell works best in the evenings after 9pm. For this spell you will need to write a list of all of the ways this person has hurt you, being nothing but honest. Then fold the paper into an envelope. Fill the envelope with mud, pepper, chili, anything nasty or gross. Write their name again on the front of the envelope. Take it and bury it somewhere away from your home. When you finish, spit on the ground where it is buried, and they should receive full karma within 3 days.

Bones to dust

The worst of all hexes. This one should be left to the absolute scum of the earth. But, if somebody came into your life and utterly annihilated you for their own personal gain, it's very much justified. For example, this is a hex I use on men that beat women. I once willed that the abuser would break a bone as he broke nine bones in his victim's face. Low and behold, he broke his leg 3 weeks later. Justified and karmically delivered. So yes, as tempting as it may be to hurt someone who has hurt you, act with caution and only practise if it is justified.

You will need:

- Dried chicken bones (oven baked)
- A plastic bag
- Dustpan and Brush

Take a photo of your target of write their name in bold back pen on a piece of paper. Put the photo or paper in the bottom of your carrier bag. Then add roughly five dried chicken bones into the bag and tie it shut tightly. Start jumping and stamping on the bones with pure anger as you scream out your intentions for your target. The bones will then turn to dust. Pick up the bag but do NOT open it. Take it somewhere with open space and then open the bag for the wind to carry the dust away. Then take yourself home and trust that your target will suffer in the ways that you have, maybe even more so.

Peppercorn Dash

An incredibly simply yet effective way of firing some bullshit at the person who screwed you over! Simply hold up a picture of your target and start dashing pepper corns at the photo. As you do so, return their karma unto them by the power of 10. That's it! This spell usually causes illness and general bad luck for the target. Just be sure it's justified otherwise you will receive the same treatment! If it's a handheld photo you've used, burn it after. If you use your phone, permanently delete that photo. You never want to hold onto any objects that you have hexed or wished negative energy onto as you will absorb it yourself. You can choose to use other things such as prunes and raisins, but I've always found the peppercorns work best.

The Irish Way

One of my best friends Nikki, who also works on the page, has a karma spell of her own. She has done this spell many times and had amazing results from it. She has very kindly agreed to share it with you all!

You will need:

- Black witches salt
- 1 Black candle
- 1 White candle
- Half a lemon
- Fresh or dried chilli's
- Black pepper
- Paper & pen
- Cauldron or fireproof dish/pan
- Matches
- A Jar
- Garlic
- If you want to also bring some healing and closure to a situation, you will also need Rosemary and Mug wort.

Set up your Alter/sacred space. There is no right or wrong way in doing this. You can add anything you desire but I would recommend having a black obsidian crystal, a rose quartz and tigers' eye but again this is optional. Call upon your guides angels and spirt to surround u with a beautiful white light of protection and to only allow light energy to enter my energy field. Call upon goddess Hecate to assist you with your spell as she's associated with both good and bad. Now place your garlic by the alter as an offering to Hecate.

Light your black candle and while doing so set the intention this candle represents all who you are involving in this spell.

Light your white candle and again set the intention that this candle represents you, peace and purification.

Write out all names involved in karma spell and burn using the black candle and place in your Cauldron. Now add a squeeze of lemon, A pinch of chilli & a pinch of black pepper. If you're adding healing and closure, add your healing herbs.

Now sit in your power and repeat:

Let cruelty pain and evil ways

Follow this villain through all his/her days.

Nothing more nothing less, reverse the torment he or she creates.

By the power of three, so mote it be.

Take a moment to visualise sending back every ounce of their negative energy and thank your spirit team for assisting you. Now take your Cauldron and empty the contents into your jar and add the half lemon u previously squeezed. Seal the jar with black wax from your candle and dispose anywhere away from your house.

Do not blow out your candles, instead stub them out. Leave to settle and then clear away after one hour. Your spell is complete!

Truth Exposure Spell

Get the feeling somebody is lying to you? Are you in a situation where the truth is being hidden and needs to be exposed? Try this spell.

Get a mirror or find a nearby window. Breath on the glass to create enough condensation. Write the person's name on the glass and then dip your finger into salt. Spread the salt clockwise around their name and say the following:

"Whatever you hide, whatever is concealed, expose it fully so that all will be revealed".

Then wipe the name away completely.

Quick, simple and incredibly effective! The truth is usually revealed within 7 days after this spell is done. Be aware, nothing will happen if there is nothing being hidden. You can then confidently take this as a sign that you can trust this person or situation.

What a flop!

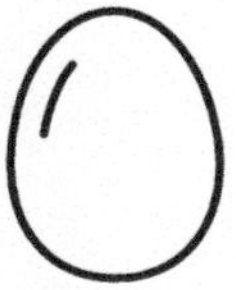

This spell is useful if you are in a relationship with or seeing a male. It can be used karmically or as a form of protection for yourself. Sexually transmitted infections are dangerous to a woman's health and her ability to conceive a child. A male engaging in sexual activity with other people while also engaging with you is a huge risk. Karmically you are justified to do this spell if your mate has declared that you are in a monogamous relationship. It will effectively stop your partner being able to get an erection for anyone other than yourself all the time you are in a relationship. In turn, it will protect you from disease.

You will need:

- One Egg
- One Needle

- One Rizla/Small paper

Write your partners full name on the small paper or rizla. You are then going to roll this paper up as small as you can get it and thread it around the tip of a needle. Then, make a small hole in the top of an egg and gently thread the paper down into the egg. This can be fiddly so you will need to be careful not to split the egg as the spell will fail. Once finished, please the egg in a freezer and leave it there. Job done!

Elemental Rituals.

Anyone from any elemental house can do these rituals. They are most powerful for the element themselves, but it works for all. Rituals are used for energy cleansing, huge spells and manifestation and to respect the spirit guides and goddesses. They can be done at any time, day or night!

BONFIRE RITUAL - Fire is powerful stuff so make sure any fire rituals are done outside in a safe place. Creating large fires using wood (never plastic or other materials) is a ball of energy and can be harnessed anyway you chose. I often use bonfires for large spells, releasing the past and praising the goddesses for their work. Use this however you chose and however feels right to you. Tune into the flames as it will also show you signs and messages (I often take photos and work out the images later). Dance, release and relax!

OCEAN RITUAL: This one obviously needs to be done on a warm day or you can even use a swimming pool. Go under the water for as long as you can and remain totally still. This will reset your thoughts and energy before you bringing you back up to the surface. Taking a long swim also helps to cleanse and recentre your chakras. It's a great ritual for fertility and dealing with health issues.

EARTH RITUAL: Into the woods we go! Take a walk and make contact with all of the trees and plants around you. Harness their energy and heighten your universal vibration. The woods are a safe place for all witches who need to retreat, make plans and heal themselves. Lie in the dirt, track water sources and appreciate the mother earth herself. You will leave feeling totally rejuvenated.

AIR RITUAL: Breathwork is a great ritual. Breathing deep, motoring and focusing on your breathing is a fantastic grounding technique for everyone. Getting outside into open spaces and letting the wind carry you wherever it takes you. Also enjoying a windy storm and screaming out into the wind is amazing for releasing and manifesting!

Chapter 5 – Divination & Tuning

Divination is the practise of predicting the future. It calls upon the universe to deliver clear messages and signs to guide and prepare us for what is to come. Tuning is the process of aligning yourself with the universe and being able to fully receive the messages of spirit guides. Both of these tools will hugely assist you in your journey of becoming a witch or spiritually awakened. There are many ways to do this but I'm going to share with you my fool proof tips on divination.

Pendulums – They are divination tools used to answer yes and no questions; they can also be used to detect spiritual presence. You can buy these online or make your own. You need a piece of string or a chain and simply attach something to the bottom that points downwards.

All you need to do is hold it steady, I usually rest my arm and let my hand relax to make sure my movements don't influence the pendulum. Ask your guides to show you what motion your yes and no is. It may swing forwards and backwards for yes, or circular for no. It is different for everyone. If the pendulum stays still or remains stuck, there either isn't an answer for your question, or the current spiritual energy is too low to use. You can test your pendulum by asking it questions you already know the answer to, just to be sure you've got the right energy going to give you correct answers.

Tarot and Oracle Cards – Now you may have heard that it's never a good idea to read your own cards. This is true to an extent as you will either only ever get one of two answers; what you really want to hear or your biggest fears. The answers are rarely accurate so ask others to do them for you. If, however you are able to emotionally detach and be open to what the cards have to say, you can use them to your advantage. I prefer using oracle cards for answers and tarot cards for general readings on upcoming events. You can get a timeline on questions using tarot cards by doing the following:

Ask your question. Pull three cards randomly. Add up the numbers of the cards. Keep pulling until you hit a major arcana or a card with no numbers. This will be when the timeline stops. If the number is between 1-30, this is days. If it shows between 1-12 on one specific card, this is usually months, but you have to use your intuition. If it's over 30, this is usually saying "not anytime soon". It can be hard to tell the difference so try pulling them a few times to get a rough idea.

There are such a huge variety of ways to use tarot cards and you can find all of them online, but it really comes down to how YOU interpret the cards and what your gut tells you!

Scrying – This method goes back thousands of years in fortune telling. There are a variety of scrying methods, but I'll explain the easiest ones. Use a bowel of water and light a candle. Allow enough time for wax to melt and then pour the wax into the bowel while mixing the water clockwise. You can ask a question or ask for general advice. The wax will create symbols and shapes for you as a sign.

Above all, watch for the signs. They are EVERYWHERE. If the universe has a message, it will not stop trying to get it to you until it smacks you in the face!

General Manifesting and Wish Spells

If I need to manifest something quickly, I have a few ways of doing this. It takes little to no effort and always comes through! As always, have full belief in the universe and be sure on your intentions. The universe loves specifics and certainty.

- What you see is what you get – Visualising technique. Literally take 10-20 seconds to imagine what it is you want to attract. Feel the feelings connected to it and then snap back to reality!
- Like attracts Like – What you are putting out there is what you attract more of. Need money? Give money. Need love? Give it. Karma is constantly in operation.
- Burning wishes – Burn your written wish on a candle using paper of bay leaves. Very quick and very effective.
- Rub your hands together to generate energy while asking the universe for what you want. Thank the universe three times and you're done!
- Put on some theatrical music that gives you goosebumps. Manifest as soon as the hairs on your arms stand up! Your vibration will be high!

Get creative with manifesting and start working out what works for you and what doesn't. This is your game of life and you are holding the controller. Use it!

Candle Communication - Fire is easy to manipulate for the spirits. They communicate with you by moving the flame in different ways. For example, if you take two candles and label them YES and NO, your spirit guides will flicker the flame of the candle with the answer to your question. Spirit guides can also send signs and messages through flames if you concentrate, you will see them.

Signs your spirit guides are present:

- Ear ringing. This can be one or both ears and it feels like you have just suffered a loud explosion! This is due to the frequency of the spirit energy and your ears are very sensitive to it!
- Smelling smoke is a clear indication of male spirit guides being present. It resembles burning wood or incense.
- Feathers are often dropped by female spirit guides to alert you of their presence around you. They are mostly white
- Coins on the floor are a spirit's way of letting you know that you have abundance coming your way! Find a penny pick it up, all day long you'll have good luck. These rhymes have meaning you know!

- Angel numbers. The universe works numerically, and your spirit guides will show you repeating numbers to let you know that you aren't alone! 111,222 and so on. You can google the meanings of these numbers if you are interested.

Magical Phrases

So, our voices were given to us for a reason. To express ourselves, to communicate, to sing... it's an important part of who we are. Our voices make our thoughts known, and of course, our thoughts control and shape our lives. Your words have power!
You must have heard the magicians saying "abracadabra!" after doing a magic trick. This is because this is a magical word! This word is an Aramaic phrase meaning "I will create as I speak". And create it does. I often say this phrase after manifesting or doing spell work and it works a treat!

So mote it be. In the simplest of explanations, this phrase is a pagan term that insists on the manifestation of what you've asked for. I usually say it at the end of every spell or manifestation and trust that it will be delivered.

"Wouldn't it be funny if…" Yep, we've all said it more than once in our day to day lives. What you probably didn't realise was that this is one of the most powerful phrases of energetic attraction there is! You are effectively challenging the universe to deliver whenever you use this phrase.

Thank you, thank you, thank you. Gratitude to the power of three is incredibly effective in spells and manifesting!

"No matter what I do, I always seem to attract abundance!" Yes, yes you do. And so, you shall. Put it out there and the universe will align with you.

Anything you say will find a way to manifest itself. Ever heard the saying "speak of the devil and he shall appear"? Its very true. Never voice something that you DON'T want to happen.

Affirmations of Power

As you now know, words have power. So, what you say about yourself and to yourself will make all the difference. Start being conscious of your thoughts, particularly about yourself. When you catch a negative, dismiss it. We all have an angel and a devil on our shoulders and sometimes it can be hard to shut the little gremlin up. These affirmations will reconstruct your mind and thought patters to attract the absolute best of energies. Try repeating these throughout the day until you consciously believe them:

- I am the entire universe. The power I hold in my hands is infinite.
- I am the granddaughter of witches and goddesses; I am a force to be reckoned with.
- I am divinely protected and only blessings flow towards me.
- Today is going to be even more magical than yesterday.
- The earth, the sky, the air and the ocean are all within me.
- Money flows to me effortlessly, I deserve financial stability.
- Love surrounds me, everyone around me can see how beautiful my soul is.
- I am exactly where I need to be in this moment in time.
- I am doing the best I can with what I currently have.

- I am constantly learning and growing, I love myself unconditionally all the way.
- I deserve everything that I want in this lifetime and I will receive it.

When you empower your body and your mind, you are in full control. Any negative thoughts that come your way, imagine them as arrows. In your mind just grab them and snap them, they are not yours and do not belong there! The mind is meant to be trained and you can control it with practise and repetition. YOU are in the driver's seat! A habit takes five days to form, so start today and begin actively creating positive thoughts while disposing of negative ones.

What to avoid!

As with all trades, there are a good number of things to avoid in witchcraft. These are mistakes I have made previously in my path as a growing witch and I'm happy to be able to prevent others from doing the same! You don't of course have to listen to me as you are your own practising witch now, but from experience, I would avoid doing the following:

- **Over doing it:** Avoid doing too many spells or manifesting too much at once. Energy needs time to settle and build after every intention is set. Give your spells the time to manifest before doing anything else. Doing too much will just congest the energetic field around you and delay your goals. Let it breathe!

- **Doing spells for others**. As a baby witch, you will need all the energy you can get. Doing spells for others at this point will drain the life out of you and impact your own spell work. Until you are totally confident in your work and understand your energetic limits, keep your powers to yourself. There is also the possibility that you do a spell for somebody and it backfires, which won't go down too well karmically (even with good intentions).
- **Multiple Sexual Encounters**. And no, I'm not "slut shaming" anybody. Do what you like sis. However, upon your spiritual journey or ascension, you are going to need to be very careful who you share your energy with and who's energy you take on. Sex is the most powerful transaction of energy there is so try to protect yourself during this time or you will become a sponge to the demons of others. Abstinence is a woman's power and provides her will full protection and health, especially during spiritual development.
- **The God Complex**. Yes, you are powerful, and you will learn this as you progress. Always stay humble and never use your powers to harm or control others. The spirit guides do not take these actions of arrogance lightly and you could lose your gifts.

- **Black Magic.** This includes hoodoo and voodoo magic. This kind of magic has great consequences and should only ever be practised by highly experienced witches. AVOID.
- **Brujeria.** This Magic can only be practised by witches of a Latina background. Even so, it requires a lot of studying to master it and also carries with it some hefty backlash.

As always, witchcraft is a bit of a mix of success and failure. But it's all a learning curve. If a spell of yours backfires, always document it and change it up next time! Just be open to being wrong and you'll be absolutely fine.

Random Magical Tips!

Here are a few of my favourite methods to surviving life, and also to keep things as sweet and positive as possible. I hope they help!

- If you need to test whether or not somebody should be in your life, use this trick. Ask your spirit guides to make them say a specific word randomly in the next 24 hours. It can be something like "pink rabbit", something they wouldn't usually say and would stick out like a sore thumb. Ask that they say this phrase to expose negative intentions or as a sign to avoid them!
- Need to boost your fertility? Carry mug wart around with you for 7 days in a red bag. It is a herb used to purify and support your ovaries!
- Already pregnant? Wearing coral bracelets are known to protect the foetus until birth and provide the mother with maternal health!
- Hit a wall? Stop all spells and manifesting. Take a cleansing bath and rest for 24 hours. Declare that your energy is pulled back to you and then start again!
- Having anxiety? Put rosemary oil on both wrists and hold them to your nose. Your senses will kick in and you'll relax.
- Feeling angry? Let it boil into your chest and scream out something you want to happen! Anger is one of the most

powerful emotions we have and works fantastically for manifestation!

- Need a sign? Look at any bookcases around you" close your eyes, ask a question and open your eyes. Look at the first book that catches your eye. Usually the title will tell you something!
- Lost something? Ask your spirit guides to reveal the lost item to you within 24 hours. Turning anti clockwise in a circle three times also helps you with memory loss and retracing your steps!
- Period or ovulation problems? On a full moon, sit outside under her glow and ask her to sync your cycles with hers. You will start to have a more regular menstrual cycle with less complications!
- Trying to attract something using written spells? Always fold the paper TOWARDS you. If you are trying to remove something, fold the paper AWAY from you!

Final Word

Right, that's all I've got for you lot so far. I'm still in the process of learning and experimenting so I'm sure I'll have another book to follow soon enough! Thank you for taking your precious time to hear the voice of just one witch in a world of many. I sincerely hope after reading this that you begin to understand how powerful and special you really are. Nobody is you, and that is your true power. Remember that all good things take time, Rome was not built in a day! Have patience with your growth as a woman and as a witch in training. Just remember, everything is intention. Whatever you set your mind too, you will achieve. You can create your own spells and rituals; all you need is the power of the goal. Become your own independent witch and enjoy the experiments! You'll win some, you'll lose some. Give it time and soon you'll grow a new level confidence you never knew you could possess. Trial and error are the basis of spell work so never kick yourself or discredit your work. Be a bad bitch, don't take on anyone else's bullshit and stay in your lane. Be unapologetically yourself and surround yourself with all of the wonders this world has to offer. Please remember that none of us have a fucking clue what we are doing floating on this big rock through space, so go easy on yourself. Develop, learn, grow every day and embrace all of life's challenges and rewards. Good things are coming! Remember I will still be practising my own spells on Instagram if you feel you would like me to do a spell for you! You can do it, and you will! And if you find yourself slipping, come and see me on a LIVE, give me a message or re-read this book.

Stay magic as fuck, always.

Love, Jess x

A Few Spell Reviews...

These reviews were written and sent to me by clients themselves. I have not changed any of the wording or vocabulary for their authenticity.

Venus spell

"I've had multiple spells from Jess the outcome all the time has been amazing. The ones I mainly use are money and self-love. The first time I done a money one about 1-2 hours later I was on my online games and was winning like £10 £25 then I won a massive amount it was mind blowing. The self-love one, wow never in my wildest dreams did I think I would ever love myself but guess what this spell worked I love me now an I'm so happy.
The Venus spell is just mind blowing the speed in which this happens an plus stays for a week is amazing. Just Little things happen like little bits of money appear, my relationship gets stronger an I'm able to achieve little goals I didn't think I could.
I highly recommend doing these spells my life has changed for the better and I truly appreciate the time Jess puts in to help an make us who we want to be.
Thank you thank you thank you!"

Tanya, Liverpool

"I had amazing results from the Venus spell that Jess did for me. I asked for money and luck and within a couple of hours of lighting my candle I already had been given an unexpected £100. A couple of days later my husband told me that he is going to be paid an extra £500. This was my first time having a spell from Jess, but it definitely won't be my last."

Those Phoenix Girls

Harriet, Shropshire

"I had a Venus spell by Jess on the full moon. The day after I had been poached by companies to go work for them which offered me A LOT more money than my current and I'm currently in deliberation in what to do. The jobs that were offered were my dream jobs since I was younger. The Venus spell also helped boost happiness and love with my man and it's still working its magic. Excited to see more results coming from this!"

Megan Conway – Derbyshire

"Around a month ago I had a Venus spell done and my life changed so much very quickly.
I was really unhappy in a salon I'm working in and I wanted to leave but I'm quite new to this area and was too scared to try go out on my own. The day after my spell a client told me of a man with a beauty room. He offered me the room straight away. My next client that day was new and a social media influencer and offered to promote my new room for free because she was happy with my service. The next day my little girl's dad offered to get me my own salon. All that week my clients shared my posts and got me so many clients from it. And a new business scheme offered me a grant and free courses. My new landlord of the salon has now offered me to go into business with him and loads more training too. Also I know it's a love spell too I didn't find love with a man but I met such an amazing friend who now I spend all my time with and my don't know what I'd do without her. My mood changed and I felt so lucky and happy. I also feel like the luck has continued. Couldn't recommend the Venus spell enough. Jess's spells work miracles as does Jess herself"

Rachel from Manchester

"I am absolutely blown away at all the results I've had overall with every spell, they have worked amazingly well for me every single spell you've done I've seen big changes!
Okay so the first ever spell I had done was a being your ex back spell, we had absolutely 0 contact for 3 months and I thought we would never speak again as we had ended on really rough terms however THAT SAME DAY that jess did my spell he messaged me and we have been speaking for the past 7 months!!
Jess did a spell to sweeten up communication with my ex and he had told me the next morning that he dreamt about me and wanted to see me as soon as possible! Our communication improved and he was being extremely sweet.

I did the Venus spell for the first time and I felt so in touch with my feminine side, I felt super confident and had a buzz of happiness it really motivated me to learn more about being in tune with my inner goddess, the spell changed me in so many ways I am grateful for! I attracted love in so many different ways but most importantly myself love increased massively all thanks to jess!

Right before I went on holiday jess did the Venus spell for me (my second time getting it) and OH MY GOD that day I was stressing not knowing if I would even make it to my holiday and I couldn't find any solutions for anything, had such a hard time looking for a PCR test and day 2/8 test. As soon as jess did the spell my best friend told me she happened to start a new job at a lab which does all the tests for really cheap! When I travelled, I never got stopped by the borders it went so smoothly and during my trip I met the most amazing guys which were my ideal man!! I was so lucky and everything went successfully I attracted love from many different guys and experienced the best yacht parties which I wasn't planning on doing at all however with the help of the spell I met the most amazing people which led to the best memories!

I purchased a love/success candle which absolutely changed my life for the time I was using it (it has finished now) but it made the impossible POSSIBLE! I mysteriously passed an exam that I know for a fact I would have failed if it wasn't for the candle, I ended up passing my first year of uni, I got amazing results for my second semester (which happened to be when I purchased the candle) and overall did attract new unexpected lovers from abroad that I've never met before and ex's!"

Rahil Saimari, Iran

"Jess I just want to thank you so much, Since having a specific spell done by yourself and receiving one of your spell candles, I literally can't believe how my life has changed in such a positive way.
I have a new job, I'm training for a qualification, I'm on good money, everything feels so positive now and also the spell you done for me a few months back I'm starting to see and Feel it materialise.
I think what you do is amazing and you're truly gifted and I can't thank you enough for the happiness and positivity in my life now.
My dreams are becoming a reality".

Leanne Elves, Washington

"I've always believed in psychics & the power of crystals, but I was less convinced by spell work... well that was until I came across Jess's work!

I have bought Jess's Venus spell twice. The first time, within 2 days, guys from my past started messaging me & on the third day, I got a completely unexpected tax rebate for £270!
I was so amazed with this outcome; I bought the spell again a few weeks later & this time I got an inheritance cheque for £12,000! I was completely blown away! This was a lady who was friends with mum... who I'd never even met! "

Janis, Glasgow

"Jess did the Venus spell for me back on the 1st of July 2021. This was a group of three spells combined. 3 weeks later I received a letter from work informing me I'll be receiving a pay rise. I can't thank Jess enough for the help, support and encouragement she has offered me since I've known her"

Leanne Spencer, Hampshire UK.

Money spells

"So, this girl is amazing, I started following Jess a few months ago on Instagram and have never been disappointed. On one post I seen that she was doing money spells so thought I'll give that a little go because who doesn't want a little extra cash! It was dead easy to be included and literally that next day I won £100 on a scratch card I couldn't believe it. So, I went on to buy 2 money spell candles from them. Every time I have lite my candles money flows to me, whether that's extra money from work, numbers on the Irish lottery or scratch cards I always get a flow of money. I couldn't recommend these girls enough"

Kandice, Liverpool

"So I had a money spell from you girls a few months back when money was really tight for me and it was really effecting my health and wellbeing, I saw how much success people were getting from your spells so I jumped at the chance to try it, within 1 week I had an email from my landlord saying due to new laws I was owed a refund of £300 on my tenancy deposit, three days later I was offered extra pay in work for the extra effort I was putting in which made another £200 all within two weeks of using the spell, honestly could not be more grateful to these beautiful girls as not only did they improve my financial situation but also my physical and mental wellbeing.

A second spell used was the fertility spell as my sister has PCOS and was told she would never have children, the miracle of conception worked within 2 days! Of the spell and now we have 2 beautiful healthy baby boys"

Laura from Aylesbury

"Well what can I say about these, it's literally in the title. Within a month of the spells I got offered an amazing job on more money, less hours & only through a telephone interview, not the whole process that was actually intended (two interviews) I won around £400 over the month through little unexpected things like some of my bills reducing, winning on the lottery etc. Will definitely be doing some more of these.
Thank you for being you, I think you're amazing!"

Becky from Gloucestershire

I purchased the success and money spell from Jess a little while back. I received my security clearance renewal through the next day after I'd been waiting for it to come through for months! I also had a big win on a scratch card and I never buy them! Absolutely incredible results!

Becky, Swindon

"I had a money spell off of Jess as I was a bit down on and out with money so thought I'd give it a go. Within a few days of the spell I had bookings coming out of nowhere for my side hustle which helped, and I thought wow it's worked but it wasn't over! A few weeks later I left my full-time job due to stress and applied for another job which was advertised at full time but would consider part time. I offered part time hours and got employed but they still gave me the full-time wage even though I was doing 10 hours a week less! I had to wait a few weeks to start. A family member knew I'd be a bit stuck so gifted me £1700 and then my old job paid my final payment was £3800 (was expecting £1300) I'd never had so much money in my account in my life even on payday!! Thank you, Jess",

Jessica B, Kent

"I purchased a money and prosperity spell from Jess and the following day On my day off from my job I was happy with I was having a meal with my family and I was offered a new job out of the blue with more money and better hours
So I took it and the money just keeps on coming!
I then purchased a Venus spell and omg I've never had so many men complement me and ask me out

I had an issue with ordering a driving licence from a third party company who charged me 3-4 times the amount of licence and that week my bank refunded me the money because the company was refusing to cancel or help
My life has changed so much since buying my first spell
Most definitely recommend absolutely amazing
Thank you Jess"

Elaine from Liverpool

"I requested a money spell, one that I hadn't asked for before as I felt there were others out there who needed it more than me, though always seen amazing results from people who had purchased! Anyway, I began a court case and started to struggle with solicitors fees, I tried absolutely everything I could to try and bring income in but I just felt like I was drowning in debt! I came to you for a money spell and around 3 days after I decided to try my luck on scratch cards, I spent £10 and I literally won my money back so I took this as a sign to wait and have it come naturally !! I put it out of my mind and around 10 days of my spell being completed I received an email from government gateway to say I was being awarded with a £538 tax rebate, 3 days after this the money was in my account!! I am so grateful for this and I am a huge believer that the more in need a person is, the better this spell will work!! I never felt like I was in a situation I would need a money spell and when I did hit that place, your magic definitely came through!! Thank you so much Jess!"

Caitlyn, Wales UK

Love Spells

"I had a love spell from Jess around 4 months ago to bring in new love. Jess worked her magic and days later My Taurus man (who Jess also predicted coming in) appeared. We are now 4 months in and happier than ever. I really couldn't recommend getting one of these spells enough and the results they give. The spell attracted the man who was meant for me and it all worked imminently"

Megan Conway - Derbyshire

"I found Jess when I split from my then husband. She offered me love spells which helped with myself love and gave me the strength to get through my separation. I also found everyone around me was more loving towards me also. She also advised me on how to become a stronger woman for me and my children. Since finding Jess I have had numerous spells from her, and they have all worked! I had an energy boost spell from Jess and all my manifestations came true that 24 hours in June. I asked for a Venus spell in June and received an email from the divorce courts informing me that my soon to be ex-husband owes me money through the divorce. The weight loss spell Jess did has worked wonders. I followed all the advice and have gone down a dress size. Jess performed a love and money spell for me on the 20th of July and within 72 hours I received £1265 in my bank account from money which was meant to be owed to me. I have also received a few luck spells and every time I have won raffles every time.
Jess's spells have helped me so much through this tough time of uncertainty and I can never thank her enough for all the help she has given me not only with spells but advice and guidance as well"

Michaela G, South Wales.

"I approached Jess for a love spell after seeing so many amazing reviews. I have been single for 6 years and was ready to finally meet a good one. I didn't have much hope after past experiences but within two weeks of doing the spell, I met my soul mate. We have been together ever since and that was just over a year ago. Can not thank Jess enough, she is a wonderful person inside and out!

Rita, London

Healing Spell

"So Jess was doing a live an done a live healing for my dad who was diagnosed with cancer a few months before he was in hospital at the time she was doing it we thought he wouldn't get out he was literally knocking on deaths door. The next day I got a phone call to say that my dad's health had improved over night and the nurses and doctors were amazed at how this had even happened. He told me himself he felt like he could run a marathon! He is still here to this day and not in any pain he was giving 9-12 months but was told he would probably go before because he can't have any treatment or surgery but he's still here and is still happy I can't thank her enough for giving me more time with my big bad Phil!"

"Where do I start, Jess you truly are one of the most genuine and highly gifted souls I've had the pleasure of meeting. Not only are u a powerful strong independent woman that helps thousands of people on their path in life you are also an incredibly gifted witch with mind-blowing results with your spell work, u done a healing spell for myself when I was in a low place and overnight I became positive with a totally different outlook on my situation and was bursting with energy and motivation. It felt like all the negativity was sucked out of me.

My son was in a serious car crash and you done a reverse healing spell on his injuries and all I can say is WOW, we were all mind blown, his bruises just vanished after a few days including his swollen black eye. Even our doctor couldn't believe how fast he healed. He was told 6 weeks for his back injury and again full recovery within days.
We are so grateful to you and your amazing gifts and still blown away by the results of your spell work.
Keep shining bright and don't ever let anyone dim your light."

Nikki, Ireland (who now works on the page with me!)

"After struggling for years with an ED (eating disorder), that got very close to taking my life on multiple occasions. I was on my hands and knees with it. I could see no way out and with the NHS stretched so far during these times getting medical help was a far cry of waiting lists.

I came across Jess on TikTok at first and watched some of her videos around her gifts, so I gave a follow on Instagram. At first, I was really reserved about where I stood on witchcraft etc as I did believe in psychics, but this was a knew territory for me. I bought candles and finally got a reading with Jess trying a few things here there with her guidance. Jess had already told me she did not know a lot about ED's however she took me under her wing and found me a spell. Got everything together followed it right down to a tea. About two weeks passed I didn't do anything that drastic to my diet, but the scales were telling me different! 5st 5 turned to 5st 12, 5st 12 turned to 6st 2. It was coming on in a matter of weeks. But not only that even my triggers weren't bothering me anymore I did not feel the need to restrict.

Clinically unless my intake had been over 3000 calories a day the rapid weight gain would never have come on this fast there was only one explanation-the spell had worked.

It wasn't that I ever doubted Jess it was just the ED had such a hold it felt like it was a part of my DNA that I would never be able to get rid of it. But I cannot thank Jess enough. She went on the hunt for something to help me or at least ease the suffering it caused me.

I don't really care what anyone has to say. Magic is real. But more to the point I was more than lucky to find a genuine witch who didn't take advantage and had my best interests at heart.

I will be eternally grateful for Jess, she gave me a fighting chance of a normal life, a healthy life. She gave my kids their mummy back. Gone has the frail, looking woman hair falling out and out has come a woman who stands in her confidence comfortably.

Thank you so much Jess!"

Humairaa, Bradford

Protection Spells

"A couple of weeks ago I messaged Jess and asked her to do me a strong protection spell for my mum and little brother as there was a lot of trouble with bullies causing lot of trouble and turning up at their house Jess was straight on the case even kindly did the spell for free which was very kind of her the spell has worked very well there hasn't been any more trouble no messages sent no knocking on the door Jess I can't thankyou you enough you lovely human being thank you!"

Kizzy, Bradford West Yorkshire

"I feel like it was March - April time Jess done me a protection spell , this spell was to protect me my mum , my brother and my son , from a person who has caused us such trauma and abuse over so many years who implemented so much damage to us , years of physical and mental abuse a man who even tried to kill my mum and still had this thing of keep showing up and finding ways to insert himself and cause us more trauma and constantly continue to mentally abuse us he wouldn't leave us alone . We literally named him the devil. We were living in fear looking over our shoulders because of him. Since Jess done this spell it's like he's disappeared out of existence and a weight lifted we have not heard from him or had him turn up on our doorsteps. It's like he's a ghost a person who no longer exists , I don't feel that fear anymore we are not looking over our shoulders constantly scared or waiting for the pin to drop , I feel protected and I'm so thankful for Jess and her powers doing this spell for me and my family thank you so much . For your protection"

Danielle, South London

You can find all of my spell reviews on my Instagram pages; I have hundreds more stored on there and didn't want to take up too many pages of this book with them!

Spells and reviews: **@PhoenixSpellwork**

Psychic Readings and Reviews: **@ThosePhoenixGirls**

Book Recommendations/References:

"The Secret" By Rhona Byrne.

"Soraya Book of Spells"

"The Dance of Anger" By Harriet Lerner

"Lunar Living" By Kirstie Gallagher

"Encyclopaedia of 5000 Spells" By Judika Illes

Images used: Microsoft Word Stock Images Icons

Fiction / Spirituality